ENDA M

COMMIT 2LEAD!

UNLOCK YOUR TRUE LEADERSHIP POTENTIAL

First published in Great Britain in 2023 by
Enda McNulty, in partnership with whitefox publishing

www.wearewhitefox.com

www.mcnultyperformance.com

ISBN 9781915635068
Also available as an ebook
ISBN 9781915635075

Cover design, internal design and typeset by Couper Street Type Co.
Project management by whitefox
Printed and bound by CPI Group (UK) Ltd, Croydon CR0 4YY

Dedicated to my wife Julia and to my mother and father, Mary and Joe McNulty, for their ongoing love, inspiration and empowerment. And to the McNulty team and the tribe of family, friends, collaborators and clients around the world who help us to live our mission to unlock human potential.

CONTENTS

INTRODUCTION

I was lucky in that I knew my mission quite early in life. When I was thirteen and playing on my club's U14 football team, the manager asked me to take over and run the training sessions. I don't think I've looked back since. Helping people to unlock their potential was a deeply fulfilling experience, and one I've been blessed to be able to continue over the last twenty-five years.

The journey I have been on since then has taken me all over the world, but the real journey has been a mental and spiritual one. I have met so many amazing leaders, so many people who have themselves made a huge impact on my life and on the lives of others.

People like Seamus Mallon, who overcame so much to help deliver peace in Northern Ireland. People like my mother, who continued towards the same goal in the face of intimidation and suspicion. People like Rory Best and Joe Schmidt, who scaled the heights in their chosen field and were instrumental in harnessing the potential of everyone around them. Historic leaders too have had a huge influence on how I live my life. People like Ernest Shackleton and Roald Amundsen, who brought out the very best in the people they led, and achieved astonishing things as a result.

This book brings together much of what I've learned over the last twenty-five years, together with contributions from a wide range of the leaders I've worked with throughout that time. Being high-performance coach with the Irish men's rugby team for seven years gave me a wonderful insight into how great leadership catalyses excellence. Rory Best, who captained Ireland when the team became the best in the world, talks about his own leadership style, and how he helped to draw together the talents of all those who played with him. Head of Athletic Performance and Science with the squad Nick Winkelman provides some wonderful insights into energy management and habit formation.

At the same time, our growing company – which specialises in helping people reach their potential – has worked with a range of highly successful leaders across a range of performance crucibles, from politics and business to education and the arts. Many of these leaders have given their time to this project. Lorraine Culligan, Group Director of People and Culture with retailer Primark talks about the courage needed to reinvent leadership in a post-pandemic world. General Manager of Intel Ireland Eamonn Sinnott talks about his own wellbeing journey, while former AIB (Allied Irish Banks) CEO Bernard Byrne explores leadership in a crisis.

To ensure that these insights are underpinned with the most up-to-date research, I've also sought the help of two leading experts in the area of leadership: performance consultant

Katrina Steady and psychologist and executive coach Dr Mary Collins. Both have been instrumental in getting this book to where it is today.

This work is divided into two sections. The first is all about self-leadership. Everything begins with purpose; it's a concept we'll hark back to throughout the book. Next we look at self-awareness and developing the qualities that all leaders need: optimism, resilience, wellbeing and empathy.

The second section builds on this foundation to explore the ways in which great leaders bring out the best in everyone else. It begins with preparation, then goes on to explore creative thinking, diversity, communication and collaboration. The final four chapters zero in on core team-building concepts: psychological safety, nurturing a healthy growth culture, dealing with conflict and developing high-performing teams.

Every time I and the team I work with help a person or a team or an organisation to achieve all that they can be, we learn something new. There's always something to learn. Always. So my journey is, and continues to be, one of continual learning. It's also been inspiring and eye-opening, sometimes difficult, often error-strewn and sometimes mind-blowing. Never boring though. Throughout it all, I've tried to be humble, curious and hungry to learn. I know I'm a work in progress, and, if I'm lucky, I'll always be that.

This book is for anyone with the same mindset, anyone who wants to grow and learn, anyone looking for the courage, energy and optimism to reach for something better – something better for everyone. This book is for leaders who want to change the game, who want to make their own moonshots, who are learn-it-alls rather than know-it-alls; who recognise that we're all on this rollercoaster journey together.

Most of all, this book is for you.

Enda McNulty, January 2023

SECTION I – LEADING SELF

CHAPTER 1:

PURPOSE

When Doing Anything Else Just Doesn't Make Sense

Kako Bourjolly is the Chris Rock of Haiti. He'd worked for a logistics company for eleven years before a heart attack made him re-evaluate his life. Heart attacks will do that. He then became what he had been born to be – a full-time comedian and actor – and highly successful in his home country. That's not what I want to talk about here, however. I want to talk about what he did in the aftermath of the Haitian earthquake of 2010. The quake hit at about 4.55 p.m. on 12 January, around fifteen miles from the heavily populated capital, Port-au-Prince. It was absolutely devastating – killing more than a quarter of a million and leaving five or six times that number homeless.

In the subsequent months, as the country began to pick itself up, Kako suddenly found that entertaining, or at least just entertaining, no longer made much sense. He felt that same sense of wrongness that he felt after the heart attack. So he did something about it.

'My first show after the earthquake, I told everybody: it's going to be free, but bring a toy. That's your ticket. If you bring a brand-new toy, you can come to the show. Six hundred people came. It was standing room only.'

Afterwards, he brought all 600 toys to an orphanage, one of the many in Port-au-Prince. There, he and his team handed them out to scores of delighted children.

It would feel nice, you would think, handing out free toys to children with nothing, right? Kako didn't feel nice. Why? Because he noticed, as they doled out cars and dolls and other plastic things, that most of the children didn't have any shoes. Those who did had toes poking out, or soles flapping off.

In his last job – the one he had left after the heart attack – Kako had been a logistics expert. His experience at that job left him in no doubt that solving the shoe problem would not be straightforward. Suppose they showed up with a lorry load of shoes but didn't have the right sizes?

'If a kid saw everyone else get a new pair of shoes, and he got nothing, that would kill him, that would kill me. I just didn't want it to happen.'

Instead, he got sheets of paper, and he and his team drew an outline of every single left foot in the orphanage. He then wrote down the name and age of the child on their piece of paper. Armed with 300 of these sheets, he went looking for donations and sourced a pair of shoes for every single child.

It sounds corny, but even now, when he remembers the faces of those children when they took delivery of the new shoes, he starts to cry.

'I'll never forget their eyes, the happiness of the kids. It will stay with me all my life.'

You don't go back to your day job after an experience like that. Well, you could go back to your day job – and maybe many people would – but Kako wasn't one of them.

These one-off drives were no longer enough. So he started something he called Kako's Kids. It's a foundation, set up to help street kids build a better future through sport and recreation.

The McNulty team was in Haiti working with one of our clients – Digicel – when I first met Kako, back in 2014. The poverty there was like nothing I had seen before. Children and teenagers begging in the streets, dressed in rags and sleeping rough. The stories they tell are heart-rending. At a time in their lives when they should be focusing on exams or football or anything else, they're struggling just to stay alive.

The first camp that Kako ran back in 2010 put 120 kids through a programme of sport and education. Since then, the scheme has blossomed. Kako and his team have built or renovated eight sporting facilities and have had a transformative impact on the lives of thousands of kids.

He says, 'You should see the difference in these kids – the difference between those who are on their second or third year compared to the new kids. Street kids, when they come in the first week, they're defensive. They're asking, "Who does this guy think he is?" By the third week, they've kicked off that shell and they become kids again. And all they want to do is play.

'I know it's small, I know it's a drop in the sea, but I never get discouraged because one day, one of those kids might become a leader in their community, they might be the next big soccer player, and when they grow up, they'll remember what happened to them, and maybe they'll help others too.'

Several of the kids who found a love of sport in Kako's summer camps have gone on to win sports scholarships to colleges in the US.

'The other day, I got a text from a kid who went to Kako's Kids. He's a great basketballer from Gonaives, which is about two hours from Port-au-Prince. I remember the first day I met him, he had no confidence and nothing to wear. He's now in his third year in college in Boston. He wrote to me, and said that thanks to Kako's Kids, he's living his dream.'

The Golden Thread

What's the thing that prompted Kako to first leave off a career that had sustained him for so long to 'do comedy', then to take on a whole new role when the quake hit?

Meaning.

Purpose. He did these things not because they made him happy or proud, or because they boosted his ego, but because they felt *right*. There was meaning in them that was absent from all of the other things he was doing. By connecting with his great WHY, he was able to supercharge his efforts and achieve so much more than he could ever have done if he had remained a logistics expert, or even, for that matter, a comedian.

When I stand back and look at the best leaders I have worked with over the years, all have lived lives with purpose, with meaning.

The people you will meet in these pages are people whose leadership journeys only really began with the discovery of purpose. And nor is the power of purpose only relevant if you're engaged in some great humanitarian struggle. Ciara Doherty, a talented young engineer from Belfast, found the strength to get out of an abusive relationship when she realised that she wanted a better life for her daughter. This is how she puts it: 'It was no longer just about me.' We'll be talking more about Ciara in Chapter 4: *Resilience*.

When Brendan McGurgan joined a company called CDE in Cookstown, Northern Ireland, as financial director, it was a fifteen-person company trading almost exclusively in Northern Ireland. By the time he stepped down as CEO in 2019, it employed more than 700 people across six continents and had revenues in excess of $1 billion. CDE Global makes wet processing equipment for the construction and mining industries – the kind of large-scale conveyors and screening machines you see in big quarries. Where's the angle here? What has the processing of sand and rock got to do with noble purpose?

The clue is in the question. Sand is actually one of the most important natural resources in the world. You almost never hear about this, but in the developing world, illegal sand dredging and mining are having devastating environmental consequences. *National Geographic* reported in 2019 that we're consuming more than 40 billion tons of sand a year, which 'is now double the amount of sediment being replenished naturally on the Earth by the sum of the world's rivers'.[1] Brendan realised that his company could actually do something about this. He and his team in CDE articulated a purpose: *Championing sustainability to create a new world resource,* and went on to develop technologies that would recycle construction waste. That innovation supercharged the company's growth.

He says: 'Defining a noble purpose changed our direction, and drove conversations which up to that point we had been too afraid to have. It shaped our culture, our marketing and brand identity. Try recruiting a star for one of your teams by telling them that you use galvanised paint, or that you sell the cheapest widgets in the business. But tell them about your purpose, about the positive impact you intend to have on the world, and that becomes a different conversation.'[2]

We're not talking about corporate social responsibility or coming up with a nice story to put on the company website. We're talking about creating a tribe of people united in a common goal. Dr Mary Collins is a chartered psychologist and professional executive coach who's worked extensively here with us in McNulty. Her doctoral research explored retention strategies for Generation Y, or Millennials, as they're more widely known. She discovered that their career goals no longer focus on getting to the top. Instead, they want to get the most out of life.

'Generation Y want their work to have purpose,' she says. 'They want to know where they fit in the bigger picture. This generation is the most socially conscious, the most concerned around the environment, around equality, around inclusion.'

Former FÁS (the Irish training and employment authority) chairman and Bristol Myers Squibb MD Michael Dempsey is a good friend and mentor. He says that his sales teams were so good at selling the cholesterol medication Lipitor that the company sent their marketing leads from the US to Ireland to discover the secret of Michael and his team's success.

'At the time, per head of population, we were selling way more than any other division in the company,' says Michael. 'We had a good marketing plan, yes, but that wasn't what was fuelling our success. What made us different was the fact that we realised we could save lives. Our sales teams passionately believed that they could save thousands of lives with the treatment. It was that simple.'

This golden thread runs through all great human endeavour, from the personal to the team to the organisation to the planet. We don't just want to be happy. We also *need* to be useful.

Clarity of Purpose

I was lucky enough to be in the room the first time Joe Schmidt spoke to the Irish rugby squad and backroom team in Carton House back in 2013. In that first hour, he laid out a vision with greater power and clarity than any leader I've witnessed in any organisation. People often tend to complicate these things. Joe made it simple. There was no fancy terminology, no elaborate phrasing, no mincing his words.

'We will have a relentless focus on doing the basic skills,' he said. 'We're going to be the best team at delivering the basics.'

He showed us footage of the basics expertly executed: a high-ball catch, clearing out a ruck, a line-out throw, presenting the ball on the ground. I wouldn't underestimate the power of showing that footage. We're a visual species. A single image can stay with you your entire life. Joe's brilliance lay not only in declaring a bold vision, but also in showing us exactly *how* it would be done. Simple, but brilliant.

'That's starting in training tomorrow,' he went on. 'We're going to work on the basics. My expectation of every player and every staff member is that we become the best in the world at executing the basics.'

And of course that vision became a reality. Ireland became the number-one team in the world in November 2018, five years after he had first articulated that vision. Joe was voted number-one coach in the world, the team was voted number-one team in the world and Johnny Sexton was voted number-one player in the world.

Now, that came down to a whole lot more than providing a powerful vision and a means to realise it – knowing the path is not the same as walking the path – but it sure gave everyone an excellent beginning. The Irish captain, and one of the most capped rugby players of all time, Rory Best, will be talking about this in more detail later in this book.

'We're going to work on the basics. My expectation of every player and every staff member is that we become the best in the world at executing the basics'

I also want to mention another great Armagh man. Seamus Mallon, who we lost at the age of eighty-three in January 2020. One of my earliest memories is canvassing for him with my parents in South Armagh when I was a kid. There could be twenty cars in his cavalcade as it wound through the narrow roads of Armagh, with my father calling over the loud-hailer fixed to the roof of our battered green Renault 18. 'Vote Mallon for MP!' Then, when we drew to a halt, this big, strong, athletic man sprang out of the leading car, his jacket swinging. Seamus always had an iron handshake and a ready smile.

The area where I grew up was a stronghold of militant republicanism, and Seamus's and my parents' party, the SDLP, believe in non-violent nationalism. This message wasn't appreciated everywhere, which meant that sometimes Seamus took a lot of abuse on the doorsteps. When this happened, he never got irate, he never gave as good as he got. He was always courteous, always polite. In fairness, getting shouted at on the doorsteps was nothing compared to what he had to deal with during his political life. He was vilified by republicans and targeted by unionists. He was humiliated, insulted and attacked more than once. During the eighties and nineties, he lived under the constant threat of death.

Seamus never left, he never gave up. During the darkest days of the Troubles, when loyalist and nationalist paramilitaries were killing indiscriminately and everyone lived in fear, this idea of everyone living together peacefully seemed, well, naive. Childish. Stupid even. But Seamus was sustained by this same vision: that those of all persuasions could share their home place.

He talked about Emain Macha, the ancient pre-Christian burial fort and once the capital of Ulster, just down the road from where I grew up. He said: 'I used to dream that Emain Macha could become a future symbol for a new Ireland and new North of Ireland, of a common Irish and Ulster identity. The old Gaelic capital ... could become the beacon of light for a new country whose people were at peace with each other.'[3]

That sustaining vision was much of the reason why he kept going, kept driving for this possibility of living in peace. And it worked. He was one of the architects of the 1998 Good Friday Agreement that brought an end to the killing that had seen more than 3,500 people die violently. The peace is not perfect by any means, and much remains to be done, but Seamus's vision no longer looks as far-fetched as it did back then.

If purpose gives you a foundation on which to build your life, vision, as Seamus says, is the beacon that will guide you were you need to go.

Nelson Mandela had a vision of life in South Africa after apartheid. Martin Luther King had a vision of a world where his children would be judged not by the colour of their skin but by the contents of their character. Kako wants to make the lives of the kids he works with better.

> If purpose gives you a foundation on which to build your life, vision is the beacon that will guide you where you need to go

What do all of these visions have in common? They seek a better world for *everyone else*. That's the first thing you need to know about leadership.

It's not about you.

In Summary

- Knowing your purpose gives you great power in your life.

- All worthwhile human endeavour begins with knowing your big 'Why'.

- All great leaders have a purpose and a vision.

- Leadership is about getting the basics right; working on them relentlessly every day.

CHAPTER 2:

SELF-AWARENESS

Know Thyself

It's not about you but it starts with you.

Paddy Courtney spent his entire career in education helping to transform the lives of the thousands of kids who passed through his school. St Vincent's Boys school in inner-city Dublin was, by almost every measure, one of the most disadvantaged in the country. When he started out as a teacher, Paddy says that he put all of his energy into his classes but quickly found that he was battling the system. If he made any progress – if he got a student engaged in his class, if they began to attend more regularly – this progress would dissipate as soon as the child passed on to the next teacher, who always tended to have a more traditional view of things. It was heartbreaking. He saw kids with great potential dropping out after a few years because every other teacher tried to push them into a rigid system that just couldn't recognise their value.

'Older teachers were burnt out,' he says. 'They used to laugh at me, or tell me I was wasting my time. They'd say, "Oh, I used to be idealistic too." When I told people which school I was working at, they'd say, "Would you not move to a better area?" The idea was that unless you taught advantaged rather than disadvantaged children, then you weren't a success as a teacher.'

Paddy may have found his purpose early in his career, but actually making it happen? Improving the lives of the kids in his school gave every appearance of being impossible. He recognised, however, that the problem lay not with the area, and certainly not with the kids, but with an inflexible education system that had a very fixed idea about what success looked like.

'To this day, you'll hear people say the good teacher is the teacher who can get them all quiet. In other words people who are good at crowd-control, not education. We'll make them shut up but we won't actually engage with the person who's in there.'

The problem, Paddy saw, lay with the adults, not the kids. He knew that what was needed was leadership, but felt that he lacked training, that he didn't have the skills to implement change. When he was appointed home-school liaison officer, however, he was given training, and one of the most powerful insights he received centred on self-awareness. For the first time, he was prompted to look at his own triggers, at his own unconscious biases.

'I was encouraged to notice myself, to know what type of person I was, and from there, to understand the perspective of other people and how to be effective in a discussion or an argument. How to get people to work with you.'

How to get people to work with you. That's a pretty solid definition of leadership right there.

Now, instead of dealing with children in classrooms, he was going out to marginalised families, talking to parents who had a very poor experience of school, and who believed that their children's experiences would be just the same. So many of these people were overwhelmed by poverty.

'I had to ask myself: "How was somebody to be most effective in such a circumstance? How could I be useful to these people? How might a person work in partnership with these parents?"'

The point here is that in order to lead, he needed to stand back and look first at what he was doing, and then at the needs of those he wished to lead.

'I realised that I had to engage with the people. I had to identify their strengths, because hidden beneath all of the poverty and exclusion, these were human beings who wanted the best for their children. How was I going to tap into that? How was I going to support that?'

Bringing People with You

He did it by asking questions and listening to the answers. He invited parents into the school, he asked them what they needed from the school, what their children needed, what could be done to improve things for everybody. This approach met with a degree of resistance from some of the teachers. Why? Because parents were not seen as helpful. Classes were run along very rigid lines; nothing had changed for years. Here's what Paddy says about that: 'If you teach the same way for ten years, you've only really got one year's experience.

'One time, after I became home-school liaison, I was talking with a teacher about one child and their difficulties in school. This teacher told me – and this would have been typical: "Just go down and tell the mother that if the child spent an hour every day doing his homework, there would be no problems." So I visited that home and met the mother, who was a lovely person. While I was there, the guards arrived at her door to talk to her other son, the eldest daughter had health problems and was unemployed and her little Down's syndrome baby was sitting on her knee. I realised that I couldn't possibly turn to her and say, "Listen, missus, what you need to do is sit down with your son for an hour every day." Instead, I said to her, "We're not sending home any homework. You're doing great to send him to school every day."'

Paddy recognised that if he had set the mother this task – of doing an hour's homework with the child every day – she would not have the resources to do it, and it would simply become one more failure, and one inextricably linked with the school.

'We had to do something different, we had to start enlisting parents as allies, we had to start working with them, telling them things that they could understand.'

Not: you need to get your kid to school on time.

Not: you need to use a particular type of copybook.

Not: you need to spend an hour on homework every day.

'We told them, "An average child in senior infants is at level 16. Your young fella is on level 4. I want to get him to level 16, and I can't do that if he's not in school." It had never been explained to parents exactly why the kid needed to be in school in the first place. Simply telling them what I was trying to do made a huge difference.'

He found out that when you engaged with the people, you found that they had huge aspirations for and deep commitment to their children. There were people in the community who were resilient and resourceful, who had achieved things in their lives. These mightn't have been academic achievements, but the point is that the parents were open and willing to engage.

'The problem was that we in education had a closed mindset. The fixed idea was that because these people hadn't gone to college, their gifts were limited. Schools operated very much in a compartmentalised way. But working with people, you found that they had a huge amount to contribute.

'When I became a principal, I spoke to each of my teachers, asking them to come out from behind their desks in the morning. This was their chance to engage with the parents, to say, "Hello, how are you doing? How is your daughter getting on?" Again, we needed these parents to be allies. They could be very sensitive if there were incidents in the class, but if the teacher met them and talked to them every day, a relationship formed. It was no longer a case of only meeting them when there was a problem.'

The Pay-off

How did all of this pay off? One of the first things that Paddy noticed was simply this: the school became a happier place.

'I discovered, too, that one of the most powerful things you could do was tell the parent that their child had ability. When I said, "Wait 'til I tell you how good your Sean is, wait 'til I tell you about his strengths," you'd see their faces lighting up.'

Paddy realised that if this new approach was to work, the school had to rethink how they measured success.

'We had to broaden out the sense of what achievement was. If we wanted to make progress, we couldn't think in terms of exam results, we had to talk about things like being engaged, listening in class, contributing, helping others, being kind, sharing, giving out the books, being pleasant, waiting your turn ... I bought a load of armbands, like the captain's armband that soccer players wear, and gave these out for achievement. They'd go home with these and parents could see that their children were being acknowledged.'

Flexibility became the order of the day. Teachers who had success in one class with a certain methodology tended to think that they had found the magic solution, one which would work with every class. It didn't, because everyone is different. Paddy had to help them see the value in flexibility, in continually upgrading your skills.

'In staff meetings, I'd put them into threes and get them to discuss something that went well and something that was a challenge. I'd get them to listen to each other. It was so important that they supported one another.'

Throughout the whole process, there's constant monitoring, constant engagement. How is this working? Is it making sense? Are we still getting value? No one gets hung up on a particular system; they're constantly evaluating, constantly asking hard questions.

Failure Is a Torch

Asking hard questions, particularly about yourself, isn't fun.

One of the many turning points in my own life came through football. I was twenty-one years old and was centre back on the Queen's University Belfast Gaelic football team. It was my last year in college, and we were playing University College Dublin in a championship game. We won and I was named Man of the Match. So far so good.

The media were there to cover the game and afterwards they asked if they could speak to me. This caused consternation in the Queen's camp.

'We can't put Enda in front of a camera. His diction is awful. No one can understand what he's saying.'

Naturally enough, this annoyed me. Who were they to decide that I was such a poor speaker? But I said nothing and let that idea sit for a few days. And with that couple of days' perspective, I realised that they were right. It was true. My accent was so strong and my delivery so poor that it was hard to make out what I was saying. And I realised then what an opportunity I had lost, and that there would likely be other lost opportunities if I didn't do something about it. At the time, it was my ambition to become a world-class coach.

The burned-out, disillusioned teachers in Paddy's school were trying to uphold a system that wasn't working, and so they failed. And when they failed, they blamed the kids, the parents – anything that wasn't them. It never occurred to them, ask: am I doing something wrong here?

Failure in itself is no big deal. It's just a part of life. How you meet and treat failure, though, that's the big deal. When I was told I was a lousy communicator, I could just have let the humiliation swallow me up. Paddy Courtney could have put in a transfer to a new school, or joined his colleagues at the bar, and laughed at the idealistic young teachers wasting their time.

But here's the thing. When you fail, you're handed a lit torch. You can use it to burn the place down, or you can use it to light the way ahead.

So I worked on my communication skills. I got a lot of help, and I needed a lot of help, but I got better. How are my communication skills now? Still pretty poor in my view. I look at world-class communicators, like Oprah Winfrey, like former Irish president Mary McAleese, like Mohammad Ali. They set the benchmark, and that's where I'm aiming, and if you aim high, you've got huge scope for improvement. I find that prospect exciting.

When you fail, you're handed a lit torch. You can use it to burn the place down, or you can use it to light the way ahead

Another thing you're going to meet a great deal in these pages: optimism. You'd be amazed at just how powerful it is.

Ever since I was fourteen years old, I've been looking for ways to make things better, and learned pretty quickly that

that starts by making myself better. In the beginning, I was focused on sport, but over time I've widened that out to include everything in life. On this long, wonderful journey we're on, I'm always looking for people – like Paddy Courtney – to collaborate with, people who can show me something new, something different, people who can help me to learn something about myself.

About ten years ago, I was asked by Intel Ireland to put together a peak-performance programme. Not just any peak-performance programme. They wanted it to be the best peak-performance programme in the world, featuring world-class experts on things like wellness, energy management and resilience.

So I went away and began my research, and in the course of that, I found Katrina Steady. She had worked with renowned resilience expert and author Dr Karen Reivich in helping to boost resilience in the US armed forces. Working out of Fort Drum in upstate New York, she spent five years boosting the confidence, focus and energy-management skills of soldiers, as well as training leaders within the military to improve the resilience of those they worked with. Since that time, I've worked closely with Katrina, creating the tools to help performers across a range of disciplines to improve their resilience. Katrina has always emphasised the importance of self-awareness in successful leadership.

'It's about knowing yourself and your own communication and behavioural style.'

She talks about Albert Ellis's ABC Model. This basically says that external events (A) do not cause emotions (C), but that beliefs (B) and, in particular, irrational beliefs (IB) do.[1] In other words, the emotions you experience and the behaviours that flow from them aren't shaped by what happens to you, but what you *think* about what happens to you. The model also states that these things are not fixed and predetermined. We can change our beliefs, and when we do, we change our behaviours.

'It's such a simple skill,' Katrina says, 'to create an awareness of your thoughts. I think that's something that we don't really reflect on as leaders. How can you expect to self-regulate if you can't explain how you're feeling in that moment?'

> We can change our beliefs, and when we do, we change our behaviours

She points out how difficult it is to support those you lead if you can't express your own feelings. 'So you need that awareness, that emotional connection, to understand the emotions that you're feeling. Only then can you begin to understand others.'

We'll be hearing more from Katrina later, but for now, I just want to zoom in on that: self-awareness. When something goes wrong, we're conditioned to get straight into defensive mode. That's the point where you've got to hold up your hand and say, 'Stop!' That's the point at which you set your ego aside and really look at how you're reacting. Really look.

You've got to know where you are in order to figure out where you need to go.

Pace Without Reflection Leads to Trouble

The same goes for organisations. I first met Ken McGrath when he was CEO of Lidl Ireland. At the time, the retailer was struggling in the Irish market. Growth had flat-lined and its main competitor, Aldi, was beating them on market share. Perhaps the biggest issue, however, was trust. The company had conducted its first ever employee survey across all of the countries in which it operated. In Ireland, fifty-one per cent of senior executives trusted the board. Forty-nine per cent did not.

Ken, and his successor Brendan Proctor, needed a plan to reverse this trend, to boost engagement within the organisation and address the mistrust that had become endemic.

Martin Bailee was chief operating officer at the time, and would become one of the internal champions of the plan we would go on to design. He explains that the trust score was rock bottom, the worst of any country in the group.

'In the past', he says, 'if an issue like this arose, there would have been the usual presentation by the board to the executive team: we're the worst, go make everyone feel better. Give them a hug or whatever. Get it done.'

That would not work this time round. What we needed was something that went a great deal deeper. The process began with a memorable two-day offsite, where we brought the board and the executive team together and began to explore the problem. For the first four hours of that session, you could actually feel the mistrust in the room. You could see the scepticism on the faces of the executive team. *Yeah, right, just tell us what you want us to do and we'll go do it.* Because up to now, that's how the company did things.

'Up to this point, the *how* was pretty unsophisticated,' says Martin. 'It was all about pressure. Give them the target and make them jump. Maybe that's a brutal way of putting it, but anyone who has come through the system would probably agree that that's how it had been. The *how* may have been effective in delivering, but frequently, we'd end up with a bolt-on solution to a bolt-on solution; there was nothing sustainable in it, and you had a lot of collateral damage.'

Trust isn't something you regain in two days. Few people spoke up at that first session. There was a fear among the leadership team that if anyone stuck their head above the parapet, they would be immediately shot down.

But we didn't give up. We kept talking, kept listening, kept trying to figure out what had gone so wrong. That engagement continued for six months. Together, working with the board and leadership team, we teased out all of the symptoms and causes of mistrust, and set about cascading a complete change in culture.

I'm going to return to this process in later chapters. For now, it's enough to understand that point: pace without reflection leads to trouble. You need to know where you are before you can get where you need to go. You need to stop and look around. At yourself and at those you want to bring with you.

Finding True North

You ask any successful leader about the role of mentoring and feedback in their success and they'll tell you that they wouldn't be where they are without it. Former Medtronic CEO and

Harvard professor Bill George runs a course called 'Authentic Leadership Development'. It's one of the most popular courses at Harvard Business School. Within that course, George has created what he calls 'True North Groups'.

Writing in the *Harvard Business Review* in December 2013, Daniel Goleman, the eminent psychologist and emotional intelligence pioneer, explains that Bill George's groups were based on the idea that self-knowledge begins with self-revelation. They provided a safe place, where members could discuss things they could not discuss elsewhere.

Bill George says, "We don't know who we are until we hear ourselves speaking the story of our lives to those we trust."[2]

Back when I wasn't allowed out to talk to the press after that match, I didn't see that as criticism. I didn't see it as some kind of personal attack. Yes, it hurt, but after a few days I realised that, actually, this was feedback, and feedback is gold. Ever since then, I've asked so many of the great leaders that I've encountered on my

> You simply won't get better at anything unless you're challenged on it, unless you're asked the hard questions

journey for feedback, for mentoring, for anything that can help me get better. Because you can't do this stuff on your own. Nobody can. Nobody *does*. You simply won't get better at anything unless you're challenged on it, unless you're asked the hard questions.

Listen: don't *not* ask for mentoring or feedback because you figure they haven't got the time, or they'd have no interest in coaching the likes of you. In my experience, the best leaders are very generous with their time, especially with those who are serious about getting better. Looking for feedback (if it's done honestly) also sends a clear signal that you're not out to protect your ego.

Just Not Good Enough

The other key point to make here is that self-leadership, which is where it all begins, isn't just about acknowledging where you're going wrong. It's also about having clear sight of what you're doing right.

Dr Mary Collins is another key figure in my leadership journey. I first met Mary when she was head of Talent Development & Learning at one of the big four accountancy firms in Dublin. I was running a workshop on high-performing teams for the firm, and what struck me about her was her curiosity, her openness and her insight into the leadership struggles of younger people in particular. Time and again, she's seen young leaders struggle with the feeling that they're just not good enough.

Imposter syndrome, as it's called, is particularly prevalent among aspiring female leaders.

'It's the feeling that you're a fraud,' she explains, 'that you will be found out, that you got lucky, but any day now, someone will tap you on the shoulder and say, "We're on to you."'

While it's predominantly an issue for female leaders, it's not an exclusively female phenomenon. Men too can suffer from this feeling that they're somehow not worthy of their achievements.

'What's most interesting in my view is that it's in the domain of high-performing individuals,' says Mary. 'People who are quite happy just being average and plodding along don't tend to experience this, but people who hold themselves to really high standards and who have a very loud inner critic, *they* tend to experience imposter syndrome.'

It's got nothing to do with external validation either. Those who suffer from it tend to be held in very high regard by everyone they work with. It's really more about the inner critic roaring in your ear.

Mary talks about one aspiring leader she coached while they were both working in that big-four firm.

'In that world, the partner is at the top of the tree, then you have the director, senior manager, manager and trainee. Getting into management consultancy is so difficult. I was working with a woman called Anna – not her real name – who was exceptionally bright. She had a first-class honours master's from a great college. She'd worked her way up to senior manager and we were preparing to get her to director level. I was doing some psychometric profiling and 360 feedback. Her line manager thought she was exceptional, and saw her as very much on the partner track. Her clients' feedback was outstanding. They loved working with her, as did her team. They said that she was inspiring, supportive and motivating. So she ticked all the boxes ... but she didn't want to go forward for director because she did not feel good enough. She did not feel like she deserved it. She did not feel confident. She exhibited all of the classic symptoms of imposter syndrome.'

Simply knowing that such a thing exists, that you're not the only one waiting for that tap on the shoulder, *that* is empowering on its own. Mary explains that the first step in breaking free of these limiting beliefs is to notice them.

'And once you notice them, it's about gently challenging them, and beginning to replace them with more empowering, positive thoughts. As I worked with Anna, I'd say, "OK, you think you're not good enough. Let's look at your performance this year." We got data and hard facts in order to really challenge those imposter thoughts.'

Often, that's not enough on its own. Mary also worked with Anna to develop her influencing and self-confidence skills (and they are skills) and focus on her strengths. She was also assigned a mentor from within the company.

'Anna worked through it and, while she never fully overcame that sense of not being good enough, she got to a place where she was in control of it, and she did go forward for directorship. Since then, she's left the firm and is now scaling the heights in a global tech company.'

Balancing the Anxiety

Mary makes an important point. You're never completely free of these feelings, these negative thoughts. You just learn to see them for what they are.

It's also worth pointing out that almost every emerging leader experiences feelings of fear and anxiety. Not just every emerging leader. Every leader.

Back in 2018 when Ireland was the number-one rugby team

in the world, Rory Best captained the side. You see him and his colleagues on the pitch, and they look invulnerable. But the truth is that they're as human, as fallible, as fragile as the rest of us. So many times, in my work with the Irish men's rugby team, I've sat down with household-name rugby players who were shaking and barely able to speak from nervousness.

Here's the truth. Rory doesn't sleep the night before a big match.

He says that the anxiety has been there since he began playing rugby. 'You learn over time that it never goes away, so you deal with it. It becomes the norm, and you actually get anxious if you're *not* feeling like that.'

He says that the key point here is that as you live, as you experience these challenges, you learn from them.

'You know that you're not going to sleep, but you also know that you haven't slept the night before other games, games in which you've performed. Ultimately what happens is you realise that the anxiety comes from knowing there are going to be massive pressure moments the next day, and there is going to be massive pressure to perform. If you've won these big moments, you know just how good that feels. You understand that you've got to get through that pressure moment in order to get that great moment. That gears you up to do it.'

'I don't agree when someone says, "Oh, they're just loving the pressure moment." I don't know too many people who love that pressure moment, but they've learned: I know what the upside of this is, and I thrive on it. There's a difference between loving something and thriving on it.'

Any time Ireland won a penalty and opted to kick to the corner, it would be Rory's job to take the resultant line-out throw, his job to launch the attack, an attack that could go either way.

'You know that if you fuck it up, that's the opportunity gone, but then you go, you know what? I know what it's like when we kick to the corner and win the line out. You hear the roar, then, if we get over that line and we score, and the place erupts, I know what that feeling is like. I know that in the past, I made the decision, I took the pressure on and we scored. That's where you balance out the anxiety. You learn that the upside greatly outweighs the downside.'

In Summary

- All transformation begins with self-awareness. To reinvent your organisation, start by reinventing yourself.
- Negative feedback and criticism can be the catalyst for growth IF you have the right mindset.
- Create your own 'True North Group'; people who can provide you with honest feedback.
- Become aware of the irrational beliefs that hold you back.
- All organisational transformation starts with a fundamental examination of what is wrong.
- Imposter syndrome is common among high achievers. What's less common is providing the coaching and support needed to overcome it.
- Even the most celebrated leaders suffer anxiety. Even Rory Best had to 'tackle' it.

CHAPTER 3:

OPTIMISM

Optimism Is a Superpower

One thing I've realised in meeting with and talking to all of the great leaders I've met on my journey is that despite the anxiety they go through, they are all optimistic about the outcome. They all believe that things can and will be better. When you think about it, it makes sense. Why would you continue to work at something if you didn't believe it could actually work out?

When I was a kid, the Troubles were part of the landscape. We knew nothing else.

Seamus Mallon talks about the local elections that were held in May 1981, right in the middle of the IRA hunger-strikes. Ten prisoners would starve themselves to death in a protest over political status. Things were about as bad as they would get in Northern Ireland at the time. People were being blown up and shot almost every day. Militants on both sides became more and more powerful, and they opposed anyone seeking peace just as viciously as they opposed each other. During that election campaign, SDLP canvassers were frequently assaulted. Seamus used to say that being able to look after yourself in a fight was something of a pre-condition of canvassing for him. The IRA newspaper produced articles which told all kinds of lies about Seamus. He received death threats from both sides. Three times during the late eighties, he was confronted with banners and signs on the roads of South Armagh, featuring a picture of a someone kneeling with a bag over his head and a masked man pointing a weapon at him, over the caption, 'Seamus Mallon is an informer'. One time, he went to the funeral of a man who had been killed by the British army. The Sinn Féin politician giving the graveside oration launched into an attack on Seamus across the open grave. Seamus said: 'It was a lonely station, to say the least, being harangued in a cemetery, in the middle of a crowd of IRA supporters, where I had come to say my prayers for the dead.'[1]

My mother, Mary, who canvassed for Seamus for years, was no stranger to that kind of intimidation. She remembers sitting alone in a caravan outside a polling station on election day, making a tally of voters. Across the road at the Sinn Féin caravan, as many as twenty men stood staring menacingly at her throughout the day.

And despite all this, people like Mary McNulty and Seamus Mallon clung to what you might call a fierce optimism. Seamus quoted Dr Martin Luther King: '…we will be able to hew out of the mountain of despair a stone of hope'.[2]

Tim O'Connor, a former senior diplomat with the Irish Foreign Service, gave a wonderful eulogy at Seamus's funeral. He pointed out that Seamus was thirty-seven years old when he was first elected to the local council. He was married, had a child and was a school principal. He already had a successful career as a footballer behind him, and was also a fine golfer and angler.

'In other words', says Tim, 'he had a rich life. In many ways, he was fully settled down at thirty-seven. But destiny had another journey in mind for him. He entered the council in 1973 because the person who was supposed to stand for the SDLP pulled out at the last minute, and nobody else would stand.'

Seamus's friend and SDLP colleague Joe Hendron used to say that Seamus lived like he played football. He would stay on the field 'til the last man dropped. In his book, Seamus says, 'I just kept going, hopeful that the human spirit of ordinary good people would triumph.'[3]

The thing is, he wasn't the only one. No matter how bad things got, there were always those who believed that they would get better.

Paddy McKillen, now ninety-eight years of age and going strong, was born in 1924 in a tiny house in Belfast, the sixth of eight children. One of his earliest memories is of his mother's body being laid out in a coffin balanced on two kitchen chairs. She died of tuberculosis when he was four years old. In his book *A Full Life*, he says that when he was a child, he was always hungry.

'Growing up in Belfast, there were constant reminders that

if you were a Catholic, you were a second-class citizen. Catholic kids were harassed by the police; Catholic schools were in a sorry state. The best you could hope for was some lousy, dead-end job. There was no hope of college, no hope of bettering yourself.'[4]

The stories that Paddy tells about the discrimination and intimidation that the Catholic minority had to put up with are shocking. And yet, he managed make something of himself. He discovered a talent for metalwork and would go on to become a skilled panel beater. In time he set up his own company – DC Exhausts – which would become one of the few sizeable employers for Catholics in Belfast. In fact, it did so well that he was approached by a Protestant businessman – Jim Law – who asked him if he would set up a DC depot in Bloomfield, which was a Protestant part of town. This was the early seventies. By then, the violence had sent the economy into decline, so that things were bad on both sides of the divide.

Paddy agreed, but knew that the only way it would work was if no one knew that he – a Catholic – was behind it. He was only too ready to employ Protestants, but the sad reality was that a Protestant venturing into a Catholic area was taking his life in his hands. Paddy and Jim set up the depot and it was a success right from the beginning.

Paddy says: 'We did fabulous business – thirty or forty cars a day. The young lads we employed were brilliant, and they just loved working for Jim. I called in every other day – masquerading as a casual observer – but there was never a problem. Jim ran the place expertly.

'I turned on the radio one morning on the way into work and learned that the Bloomfield depot had been bombed. In spite of all of our precautions, the UDF or one of these Protestant military organisations must have found out that I was the owner. No one was hurt, thankfully, but the place was half destroyed.'[5]

The venture had been so successful that Jim and the crew who worked with him begged Paddy to try again, so he did. They rebuilt, refurbished and reopened. Within a week, the place was bombed again. This time it was completely destroyed.

At this point, Paddy gave up. There would be no new depot in Bloomfield.

Was this a failure of optimism? Should he have gone back and rebuilt a third time? Thinking about it, I realised that if he had done that, chances are it would have been bombed again. And if it was bombed again, the chances of someone being killed or maimed would have been much higher. The fact that the place was bombed twice with no loss of life was amazing really. To risk it a third time would have been reckless.

But in actual fact, Paddy didn't give up, he just changed tack. He did what he was good at, which was business. He expanded into the south, and became one of the most important funders of the SDLP throughout the seventies, eighties and nineties. In 2017, he and his friend Mackie Moyna – another successful businessman and SDLP member – were awarded the inaugural John Hume Peace Prize. By this time, John Hume himself had, sadly, developed Alzheimer's, but his wife Pat wrote Paddy a letter:

'At the most difficult times, it was crucial for our politicians, who were ploughing a very lonely furrow during the seventies and eighties, to know that their messages were being heard and that the uphill work was valued. The violence of those years broke many hearts and destroyed many lives. Many were frightened into silence by the intimidatory atmosphere of those years. The support of friends like Paddy and Mackie did so much to keep hope alive and to sustain those who spoke out against the fearful conspiracies of violence.'[6]

Seamus Mallon wrote the foreword to Paddy's book, and in it, he said of him that he took misfortune by the neck and squeezed every last drop of adversity out of it.

Endurance

That's the essence of optimism, isn't it? Grabbing misfortune by the neck. Refusing to accept that the bad times won't end. This is something I've seen time and time again with successful leaders. They see the silver lining and steer a course straight for it.

One man whose experience I turn to again and again for inspiration is polar explorer Ernest Shackleton. In 1914, he and a hand-picked crew set sail for Antarctica on a ship called *Endurance*. They never got there. The boat became trapped in pack ice, which pulled them 2,000 miles off course before completely destroying the boat.

He took misfortune by the neck and squeezed every last drop of adversity out of it

'I cannot describe the impression of relentless destruction. The floes, with the force of millions of tons of moving ice behind them … It seemed like the end of the world.'[7]

In the months that followed, Shackleton and his men, including veteran polar explorer Tom Crean, endured unimaginable misery and suffering camping out on treacherous, drifting ice floes. One night, while they slept, there was a sudden crack in the ice and one man was dumped into the water. Shackleton reacted quickest, grabbed the man's sleeping bag and pulled him clear just before the gap in the floe closed again like the jaws of a vice. The men remained trapped on the ice from October all the way through to April. Snow confined them to their tents for weeks at a time. They became weaker and weaker as food and fuel ran down. In his book *Seek the Frozen Lands*, Frank Nugent says this:

'Shackleton maintained morale by continually rearranging the menu, such as it was. One day it was seal meat fried in blubber, the next day stewed with dried vegetables. Combining it with dried milk, flour, sugar and tea also made a difference. Shackleton never claimed any privileges for himself as master and gave the appearance of confidence that they would all survive.'[8]

Think about that. Death hung over them continually; I mean, if you were a betting person, what chance would you give any one of them of survival? And yet Shackleton maintained his optimism all the way through. As the ice began to break up late in the spring, they used the three small boats that they had salvaged from *Endurance* to make it to Elephant Island, which was barren and completely uninhabited. They had drifted so far in the pack ice that no one would have any reason to look for them there. Their only hope of rescue, Shackleton knew, was to take a small group of men in the largest of the three small boats and head for the nearest inhabited outpost. This was the whaling station on South Georgia, which was 800 miles away – 800 miles of the stormiest, roughest seas on the planet. On Easter Monday 1916, Shackleton, Crean and four others set out on that now-famous open-boat journey. It is a remarkable feat of teamwork and leadership that those six men made it to South Georgia. Then Shackleton, Crean and Captain Frank Worsley travelled across the island for three days to reach the whaling station on the far side. Ultimately, a rescue party made it to Elephant Island to take on board the rest of the crew. Nobody died. They didn't lose a single man.

There's no doubt in my mind that if Shackleton hadn't believed that they could save those men, there's no way he could have led in the way that he did. And there is no way they could have followed him in the way they did.

Because calm is contagious.

To return again to that core point: it's not about you but it starts with you. The best leaders I've seen over the last

Calm is contagious

thirty years – and this is in sport, in business, in everything – are the ones who simply don't panic. Or at least don't *seem* to panic. When crisis hits, all eyes swivel to the leader. If she can't meet their eyes, if she doesn't hold herself tall and confident and calm, everything crumbles.

During the COVID crisis, I learned so much watching the

leaders we work with react to the sudden economic shutdown and all that came with it.

Lorraine Culligan is a board member and Group Director of People and Culture with Primark. The clothing retailer began in Dublin in 1969 and now employs over 70,000 people in 403 stores across fourteen countries.

Lorraine describes the events of March 2020 as the most frightening she's ever experienced.

'Why? Because we didn't have the answers. The last of our markets to close was the UK. I remember that day so clearly. Everybody was at home, all 70,000 of our colleagues. When I look back now, I think the biggest thing from a leadership perspective was staying calm.'

Staying calm. It sounds easy, she points out, but it isn't, not when your revenue dries up overnight, when you have no idea when you will be able to open your doors again and when so much about the virus itself was still unknown. Lorraine talks about the overwhelming sense of responsibility she felt for everyone who worked for the company.

'It really grounds you when your business is on its knees, you've got no revenue coming in and you have to fight to save it. But that's exactly what we did. It became all about rolling up the sleeves and getting into operations mode.'

Throughout the crisis, we worked closely with Dr Mary Collins to help leaders plot a path out of crisis. She talks about emotional contagion and the pivotal role leaders play in setting the emotional benchmark for the team.

'If I'm doing a briefing with my team,' she says, 'and I'm stressed to the gills, anxious and uncertain, that will trickle down to my team.'

I take her point. But does that mean you protect them from the truth? Is it your responsibility as the leader to bottle up all the stress and promise them everything's going to be fine?

Not at all, she says. Don't fake it. You never fake it.

'You say: "There are lots of unknowns out there, lots of uncertainties, but we've a fantastic team, we've got great talent here and we are going to navigate our way through this."'

You don't fake it to make it. There's such a thing as toxic positivity, where you suppress the negative emotion and deny that anything bad has happened. A 2013 study by the Harvard School of Public Health and the University of Rochester showed that people who suppressed their emotions increased the risk of premature death from all causes by more than 30 per cent.[9]

The key point here is you can't just present a front. Optimism has to be realistic. It has to be *grounded* optimism.

When you look at the *Endurance* story, Shackleton's optimism as he and his crew watched their ship crushed under the ice looks delusional. The fact that they survived at all seems miraculous. But if you look a little harder, you'll see that actually, it wasn't. Actually, Shackleton's optimism was realistic.

This was his second trip to the Antarctic. Nine years earlier, he was part of the expedition that made it to what was, at that time, the furthest south any human had ever gone. This was Tom Crean's third trip to the Antarctic. During the 1911 *Terra Nova* expedition, Crean had hiked solo for thirty-five miles across the Ross Ice shelf to save the life of another sailor. Frank Worsley, who was captain of the *Endurance,* was a seasoned sailor, as were most of the crew. These men were chosen because they were experienced and resourceful. It wasn't as if Shackleton was stranded on the ice with a gang of raw recruits. And what's more, many of these men were just as capable of seeing a way out as Shackleton was. Another Irishman, Timothy McCarthy from Kinsale in Co. Cork, was one of those who volunteered to make the open-boat journey to South Georgia.

To return to another core point: you can't do it alone. You need good people around you. So when Shackleton stood on the ice, watching his ship getting destroyed, he could look around and say, 'Well, if you have to be stranded on an ice floe in the southern ocean with polar winter coming on, these are the people you'd want to have with you.'

And if I look back on my career, at those low points, when the darkness was closing in, I see the same pattern. At half-time in the All-Ireland final in 2002, we were four points down and playing badly against a Kerry team that had broken our hearts over and over again. Manager Joe Kernan stood up and talked about how we could win, and so did other formidable leaders on the team, men like Kieran McGeeney and Paul McGrane. As they spoke, I looked around at the people I'd fought so hard alongside over the years and I knew – we all knew – that we could do it. That awareness fuelled our second-half resurgence and ultimate victory. And if I think about all of those people who eventually delivered peace in Northern Ireland, it was because they surrounded themselves with people – like my mother – who believed, as they did, that it was possible.

This Too Will Pass

When Bernard Byrne took over as CEO of AIB (Allied Irish Banks) in 2015, we worked with him and his leadership team, helping to bolster their fitness, wellbeing, resilience and leadership skills in preparation for the bank's IPO in 2017. Helping a high-performing team to realise their potential in what was a tough sector was a wonderful experience for us.

A few years earlier – in 2010 – Bernard had joined the bank as its chief financial officer. At the time, the banking sector was on its knees. The global financial crisis and the collapse of the Celtic Tiger economy had generated huge levels of problem debt. The first year in the job, he had to announce losses of €10 billion.

Bernard is well aware of emotional contagion in these circumstances, and believes that the first step in making sure you're spreading calm rather than panic is self-awareness. It starts with you. The good leader learns through experience how they react when the shit hits the fan. What follows from self-awareness? Self-regulation. You stand back, you sense the rising panic, but you don't allow it to climb into the driving seat. Because, as Bernard points out, if the leader is panicking, then everyone is.

I agree with Bernard when he says that sometimes people are slightly offended when you don't panic. *Don't you understand how serious this is?* He points out just what a colossal waste of energy panicking is. And anyway, when you panic, your focus is exclusively on the consequences of the problem rather than on the problem itself.

He talks about how bad things were when he took over the CFO role in 2010. 'The bank looked like it was going to disappear, the economy was completely destroyed. You had 20,000-odd employees in AIB and most of them thought they were going to lose their jobs. Customers were going absolutely ballistic, everyone in the media hated us.'

How do you handle something like that? How do you lead people when things are that bleak? Seriously. Stop reading and think about that. What do you say to your team when you know they'd leave if they could?

This is what Bernard used to tell his team.

'Listen. No matter how bad it gets, no matter how horrible this experience is today and no matter how appalling you think it is, tomorrow is going to be worse.'

OK, it's gallows humour, but it's humour, and it has a disarming effect. Look at what it communicates. The leader is not denying that there's a problem, but he's not getting upset about this. Is this a lack of optimism? On its own, yes, probably.

But then Bernard would say, 'But at some point, it's going to get better. Can't tell you when but it is going to get better. This too will pass. Everything passes. Our job is to be resilient, to get through it and not get down when Tuesday turns out to be worse than Monday and we didn't think Monday could ever be beaten.'

The point is that solving serious problems takes time. Quick fixes only work on the *consequences* of serious problems, and only work in the short-term. He points out too that everyone overestimates what can be done in one year and underestimates what can be achieved in five.

Take queues in bank branches. These used to be a huge problem. There were few things a customer hated more than having to give up half an hour or more of their day to stand in a bad-tempered bank queue.

'Queues in the branches used to be a huge issue and everyone came up with thousands of things that looked like solutions, but they all involved sticking more people into the branches. The real issue, however, was that the processes were very poor and labour-intensive. Everything was paper-based and error-prone.'

Quick fixes only work on the *consequences* of serious problems, and only work in the short-term

Bernard realised that fixing the problem would involve deploying additional resources all right, not to the branch but to the process centre.

'One of the things we focused on was how to be more useful to customers in the short *and* long term. That was the key thing. How can we be more useful? How can we be easy to use?'

In time, the core problem was solved and AIB's online banking solution became the market leader. Now, as Bernard is quick to point out, not everybody loved everything about it. There were job losses, there were branch closures. But the process improvements made the bank much easier to deal with, and the queues disappeared.

When people recognise that you are tackling the problem, that's when you can see the optimism in action. Yes, this is bad, but I believe we can make it better. Actually better, and for good. That's what I call *courageous* optimism, and courageous optimism plays a key role in developing a vital leadership skill. Resilience.

In Summary

- Courageous optimism is an essential leadership attribute.

- Shackleton's outrageous optimism kept his crew alive for months. Imagine the impact this kind of optimism could have on your crew.

- 'Most people overestimate what they can achieve in one year and underestimate what they can achieve in five.'

CHAPTER 4:

RESILIENCE

Being There for People, and Expecting the Worst

We used to think of resilience as a rare quality, something which only existed in a handful of almost superhuman people. The kinds of people they make movies about. They could suffer all kinds of hardship and still come through to win against the odds. We now know, however, that resilience – the ability to bounce back from adversity – isn't a fixed quality. It's actually a renewable resource. It can be developed. It can be taught.

Much of what we now know about resilience stems from work done by positive psychology guru Martin Seligman at the University of Pennsylvania. In 2008, Seligman had a visit from Colonel Jill Chambers, who was head of a Pentagon programme for supporting US army veterans. She told Seligman: 'We do not want our legacy to be the streets of Washington full of begging veterans with post-traumatic stress disorder, depression, addiction, divorce and suicide. We read your books and we want to know what you suggest for the army.'[1]

In the months and years that that followed, Seligman would go on to work with the US military, trying to create an army 'as psychologically fit as it is physically fit'.

Katrina Steady worked as a military resilience trainer on one of these programmes, helping US army rangers, combatives and cadets to perform at their best in situations that were high-stress and chaotic. She also ran 'train-the-trainer' resilience programmes for military leaders.

Cultural transformation doesn't happen overnight. On one of her first 'train-the-trainer' sessions, Katrina recalls walking into the lecture hall to be confronted by 180 stony-faced military leaders.

'They've all got their arms crossed. They're sitting back looking at me like there is no way they're going to take this stuff seriously. The attitude was, "I've been in the military for fifteen years and nothing you tell me is gonna change the way I lead."'

By day five, however, attitudes had changed dramatically.

'They had thought it was all rainbows and flowers, but we were able to present the cold, hard research, which demonstrates that this stuff does actually work.'

Anxiety levels soared during the COVID-19 crisis, and our resilience skills were sorely tested. From my point of view, one of the most damaging aspects of the whole thing was social isolation. Us humans can put up with a great deal, but when we are cut off from each other, it's nearly impossible to flourish.

As far back as 2010, psychology professor Julianne Holt-Lunstad published a piece of meta-analysis, which found that lack of social connection was as bad for you as smoking fifteen cigarettes a day or having an alcohol problem. According to her analysis, social isolation is twice as harmful to physical health as obesity.[2]

I believe that having a support network is absolutely crucial to bouncing back. Time and again I've seen just how important other people are in maintaining resilience. Again: you can't do it alone.

Similarly, if you are going to create a resilient team, you need to be able to provide them with the support network that will allow them to flourish in a world that is constantly throwing obstacles in their way. During the COVID-19 pandemic, it was the companies that adapted to the rapidly changing circumstances that not only survived, but thrived. How did they do it? **Having a support network is absolutely crucial to bouncing back** Through the resilience of their people. There are so many examples of this, but I want to zero in on just one.

In Apple's Q4 2020 earnings call in October 2020, CEO Tim Cook laid much of the credit for the company's record-breaking year on the resilience of its teams.

He said, 'Even though we're apart, it's been obvious this year that around the company, teams and colleagues have been leaning on and counting on each other more than in normal times. I think that instinct, that resilience, has been an essential part of how we have navigated this year.'[3]

In 2020, the company recorded revenue of $274.5 billion, fully 6 per cent higher than the previous year.

The bottom line here is that your resilience and that of your team depends heavily on how you support one another. In my experience, there is no bigger determinant of how resilient, and therefore how successful, you will be.

Reaching Out

Nobody plans to end up in an abusive relationship. Ciara Doherty grew up in a very loving home and yet, at 17, she moved in with an older man who began physically and mentally abusing her.

'Outwardly, I appeared full of confidence, but inside, I was a much smaller person. I think that this is a common experience for people in abusive relationships. And this was my first experience of love; I was prepared to do anything to make this person love me back.'

She would go on to become pregnant twice but miscarried on both occasions, the second time as a result of an abusive incident that put her in hospital.

Even after that, after going home to her family to recover, she still went back to the same man. She still turned to him for hope, companionship and love, and became pregnant again. This time she gave birth to a beautiful baby daughter. That was the turning point. That was when she knew she was in the wrong relationship.

'Throughout that time, I was studying civil engineering in college. I grew up in a family of joiners and builders, and used to help my dad when he was doing odd jobs around the house. I originally wanted to be a bricklayer or a carpenter but it was Dad who encouraged me to go the professional route and become an engineer. I loved it right from the beginning. After my daughter was born, I used to bring her into lectures and have her sleeping in the car seat beside me while I took notes.'

You would think that having a baby would make it harder to get her degree, and it did in many ways, but her daughter was the spur. It was no longer just about Ciara. Getting a degree meant getting a decent job, which meant independence, which meant getting out of the awful situation she found herself in. Her daughter gave her the purpose she had been lacking up to then. So she worked hard, studying late into the night and during lunch in the part-time job she had to get. Ciara always had her books with her and took every opportunity she had to study.

But it was all too much. The pressure of being a new mum, the abusive relationship, the lack of sleep and the stress all came to a head during her finals, on the morning of her structures exam.

'I remember sitting there, staring at the paper and going completely blank. Next came the palpitations, the shaking and the sweating. I could hardly breathe. Ten minutes into the exam, I stood up, went to the bathroom and locked myself in. I sat there, thinking, *I can't do this, I can't do this, I just can't*. What could I do? I left and went home.'

When the results came out, there were no surprises. She got 14 per cent. Total failure. She had come so close to securing her degree and all that it represented, but in the end, everything had come tumbling down. She was devastated.

Ciara's next move was, in my view, the most important one.

'That's when I began reaching out to people, that's when I finally admitted that the facade I projected – that everything was under control – was just that. I could no longer do this on my own. I reached out to my family.'

By coming clean, by being honest and sharing her burden with the people in her life who only wanted good for her, she began to turn things around. Her partner encouraged her to forget her engineering ambitions. He said things that sounded supportive, like, 'You don't have to put yourself through this,' but now she recognised that this advice was not coming from a place of love but a place of control.

So she got in touch with her lecturers and found out that this wasn't the end of the road, that she could re-sit the exam she had failed.

'Over the eight weeks between the failure and the re-sit, I redoubled my efforts, I did everything in my power to make sure that I would do nothing short of my best. My baby girl remained the motivational force. She was the why. With a degree, I could find decent employment straight away. Without it, I would be stuck in a part-time job with very little income, unable to support her, unable to escape.'

'I'll never forget that exam. Everything clicked. It was like I had a photographic memory. I remembered everything I'd ever read on structures, every note I'd ever scribbled down, every word, every calculation. I was in the purest state of flow, I hardly had to think. Everything came automatically. When I left the exam hall that day, there was no doubt in my mind that I had passed.'

When the results came out a few weeks later, Ciara learned that she had achieved the highest result ever in that subject in Northern Ireland. The post brought a second envelope that day – a letter from the Institute of Civil Engineers, saying that because of that result, she had won their graduate prize, to be awarded at their annual dinner in the Europa Hotel in Belfast. She'd never been to a black-tie event before, and was actually intimidated by the thought of it. But she went along, met some of her lecturers, had dinner and sat there, half petrified, one of only four women in the room.

'When I was called up on stage to receive my prize, I felt more embarrassment than pride; I had never enjoyed being the centre of attention. I remember sitting back down and planning my exit. How soon could I leave without appearing rude? It was only in the taxi on the way home that I opened the envelope. I had expected a certificate, something I could frame and put on the wall. It wasn't a certificate, it was a cheque, a cheque for £1,200. After the shock had subsided, I remember thinking, *I earned this, I deserve this. I'm going to make this work for me.*'

A few days later she put her baby girl to bed knowing that it would be the last time she would ever put her to bed in that house. Ciara got up in the middle of the night, packed a bag, lifted her out of the cot and left.

'In that instant, I felt free, I felt like I was in control. I had no regrets; I knew I was doing the right thing. What seemed like a huge decision was actually a simple one: just walk.'

The next challenge was to go out and get a job. Not so easy when you're a single mum living at home with a small baby.

'If I had any doubts about this, five or six interviews later made things crystal clear. I was asked questions they'd never get away with now, all of which boiled down to this: how do you expect to work fifty hours a week in a male environment as a single mother? I told them all the truth, which was that I would work eighty hours a week to provide for my little girl if that's what it took, but nobody bought it.'

The last interview she had set up was with a company called Lagan Specialist Contracting Group. This time, she planned to say nothing about her little girl. She would just tell them she was an engineer with a first-class honours degree. What else did they need to know? In the end, however, she didn't cover anything up.

'I felt I wouldn't be authentic, I wouldn't be true to myself if I pretended she didn't exist. So I told the truth, but Lagan saw things in a very different light to all of the other companies. They didn't see a single mum with divided loyalties, they saw someone with the resilience and time-management skills to achieve a first while looking after a small baby.'

Overcoming Negativity Bias

It's not the obstacle. It's your attitude to it.

Remember Albert Ellis's ABC model? The basic idea is that external events (A) do not cause emotions (C), but beliefs

(B) and, in particular, irrational beliefs do.[5] Katrina Steady reaffirms just how important optimism is in your ability to respond to adversity, but adds that becoming optimistic isn't easy. You might decide to try to look for the good in a situation, but negativity bias is a powerful force and won't be overruled easily.

'That's why you have to *continually* ask yourself: what can I control here? How can I be more hopeful? That alone is enough to help people to get to the next stage of resilience.'

The other point here is that people will often dismiss the idea of optimism by saying, 'Me, I'm a realist.' That's great, but that doesn't get you off the hook. You still have a responsibility to find the things that you can control, the things you can influence.

'*That's* what we want to hear from a leader,' says Katrina. 'We want to hear, "OK, here's where you need to focus your attention. Here's what you can do about the situation. Now go forth and do it, and let's be hopeful that we can get through this together. It's going to suck. It is going to be challenging, but you can still be optimistic about it and set out to control the controllable."'

The point here is that it's not enough that you develop your own resilience. You've also got to offer your team, your people, your community the right conditions for the growth of their own bounce-back-ability. A vital part of that is being a key figure in their support network: being the person who they reach out to when things go pear-shaped. If you want one takeaway from this book, it's that. If crisis happens and your team is afraid to tell you, or they try to hide the truth, or feel they cannot take risks or be seen to fail, it's on you.

You're the one who catches them when they fall.

Prevailing Over Tragedy

My best friend when I was a kid had a cousin called John Moran. He lived in Rockaway Beach, New York, and like a lot of Irish Americans, he was a fireman. He came back to Armagh once during the 1980s. That visit has gone down in local legend, because he just showed up one day on his bike. He had cycled all the way from Dublin.

> If crisis happens and your team is afraid to tell you, or they try to hide the truth, or feel they cannot take risks or be seen to fail, it's on you

John was one of those people everyone else looks to for inspiration. He was a big man. Six foot three, 230lbs (104kg). Both he and his brother Mike went to St Camillus Grammar School in Rockaway, where John excelled. He was also a great musician. On Memorial Day, he was one of the two trumpeters selected to play 'Taps' – which is the standard tune played at US military funerals. Mike says that every year this happened, their mother would bawl crying.

It wasn't easy to join the fire department. Every five years or so, there would be a general call for applications. Upwards of 50,000 people would take the test, but only 10 per cent would make it through. John was one of those. He came top of his class and was valedictorian on graduation day.

Sadly, John was one of those who died on 9/11. His last

words to his driver before he ran into the South Tower were 'I'll go in here and see if I can make a difference.'

In the department, John always had particular respect for those who had gone before him. By the time he graduated from the fire academy, power tools were used for cutting holes and creating the access needed to fight fires, but he got the older guys there to show him how it used to be done – with axes. 'You can't always count on power drills,' he used to say.

John quickly got onto a leadership path within the department. He went to college while working, then law school, and again graduated at the top of his class. You've also got to take tests to achieve promotion in the department, and within a few years John became lieutenant, then captain, then battalion chief.

He was hugely committed to his job. In June 1999, a captain in John's department was killed in a fire in Howard Beach in Queens. He got trapped in the flooded, junk-filled basement of a house that had caught fire. After inhaling smoke for some minutes, Captain Vinnie Fowler went into cardiac arrest. He was a big man, and the space was very tight. The water had saturated his gear and his protective clothing, and this made it really difficult to get him out. It took the team nearly thirty minutes, by which time it was too late. The loss devastated John, but he was determined to learn something from it. He said, 'We've got to come up with something, we can't let this happen again.' So they did come up with something. The team devised a way of tying up a fireman who'd become trapped or unconscious so that their heavy clothing wouldn't count against them. 'We drilled in it constantly,' says Mike, 'over and over again.'

That's the thing. There's always something you can learn, even from the worst situation.

Expecting Pitfalls

In pursuing any plan, there's one thing you can be sure of. Things will go wrong. If you set out to climb Everest, you can bet your bottom dollar that there are going to be falls, that your rope may slip, your karabiners may break, that someone in your team may get frostbite, that your tent may blow down in the middle of the night, that bad weather may force you back to base camp before you reach the summit. One or more of these things may happen, and the team leader who has anticipated these setbacks and come up with a Plan B is the one who is most likely to succeed.

Those who don't anticipate obstacles are more likely to fail to overcome them.

If you're leading a start-up and your funding falls through, or a new competitor undercuts you, or a new technology threatens to make yours obsolete, being able to pull a Plan B off the shelf allows you to make lemonade out of those lemons. It allows you to stop and say, 'Right, the situation has changed, but the goal has not.' You sit down, carefully analyse the new circumstances and find out how it affects you. Then you amend your plan and get going again.

Planning for disaster sounds negative. If you anticipate that things are going to go wrong, aren't they more likely to do so?

This isn't my experience.

In sport, the manager who has developed a plan to deal with every contingency – going ten points down, a key player becoming injured, a key player getting sent off – they're the ones who are far more likely to succeed. Why? Because at every turn, they're identifying the controllables and grabbing hold of them.

At half-time in the 2011 Heineken Cup Final, the Leinster team was losing 22–6 to Northampton. At the time, I was performance coach with the team, and it looked as bad as it could look. The players were getting destroyed in both set pieces and open play. Several people spoke during that half-time break. Greg Feek was scrum coach at the time – he now holds the same role for the All Blacks. He diagnosed everything that was wrong with the scrum, and showed how it could be turned around. Head coach Joe Schmidt spoke calmly and with his usual clarity about getting the basics right. Fly-half Johnny Sexton delivered the power speech, re-affirming Joe's points and emphasising the importance of getting the next score on the board. When the team came back out on the pitch for the second half, everybody knew exactly what he needed to do to stop the rot and fight their way back into the game. Johnny went over for a try within the first four minutes. By the end of the game, Leinster had clocked up twenty-seven points, to win by eleven on a score line of 33–22. It was one of the greatest comebacks in the history of Irish sport, and it showed just what can be achieved when you set out to control what can be controlled.

This idea, of identifying what might go wrong and planning for it, was also explored by German psychologist Dr Gabrielle Oettingen. She found that thinking positively about an upcoming challenge can actually be counter-productive. In *Rethinking Positive Thinking,* she details an experiment in which one group of college students was asked to envisage a wonderful week – full of great parties and great grades, while a separate group was asked to record their thoughts, good and bad. The students who were urged to think positively about the week ended up far less energised and achieved less with their time than the second group.

She says, 'My research has confirmed that merely dreaming about the future makes people less likely to realise their dreams and wishes ... The pleasurable act of dreaming seems to let us fulfil our wishes in our minds, sapping our energy to perform the hard work of meeting the challenges in real life.'[6]

Dreamers, she points out, aren't always doers.

She discovered that those who put time into thinking about *what can go wrong* were far more successful. And not just thought about it, but developed a plan to overcome it. If X happens, then I'll do A. But if Y happens, then I'll do B.

So here is another key ingredient of resilience. By pre-cooking a response to the things that can go wrong, you are far more likely to stay on track. Planning for a setback allows us to steal back control when it looks like circumstances have taken it away.

> Planning for a setback allows us to steal back control when it looks like circumstances have taken it away

The best way to make all of this work? By being at your very best.

In Summary

- Resilience is not a fixed quantity, it can be developed.

- A great support network is essential to becoming more resilient.

- Fortitude and resilience are essential for making a fresh start.

- The obstacle isn't important, but your beliefs about it are.

- Leinster faced massive adversity, but found the resilience and mental toughness to overcome that adversity. What about you? Can you develop the mental toughness to overcome the challenges you face?

CHAPTER 5:

WELLBEING

Unlocking the Energy for Great Habits

We all know it's important to exercise, to eat well, to hydrate and to make sure rest and recovery are as good as they can be. There are endless social media posts, podcasts, books, newspaper articles and TV programmes telling us how to live healthier lives. But it just doesn't happen.

Why is that?

Why is the gap between knowing and doing so wide? And what can be done to narrow it?

That's what I want to get at in this chapter. How do you take what you know to be good, and make it happen?

I knew within five minutes of meeting Nick Winkelman that he would become another key figure in my own leadership journey. Nick is head of athletic performance and science at the IRFU – the Irish Rugby Football Union.

'I was one of those kids', he says, 'who struggled with weight, and didn't have the thickest of skins when I found myself on the wrong side of a joke. That said, I had always aspired to look on the outside the way I felt on the inside. I think this is true of damn near everybody. Maybe it's not losing weight, but it's some other habit that somehow misaligns. There's something wrong, something that drives people to say, "I want to change."'

Knowledge wasn't an issue. At fifteen, Nick knew, as everyone does, that broccoli beats burgers. And he knew too just how important physical activity was. But here, he ran into a problem. Despite the fact that he played numerous sports, and played them well, he was still carrying too much weight.

Knowledge wasn't an issue. At fifteen, Nick knew, as everyone does, that broccoli beats burgers

So he realised early on that physiologically, everyone is different. 'I didn't eat badly,' he says. 'My family cooked breakfast, lunch and dinner. I was playing all these sports, and yet there I was, this chubby kid. And I'm looking at all these kids eating the burgers and the fries, and they didn't share my struggles.'

This is a perennial source of frustration for so many of us. Others can have terrible behaviours and don't put on an ounce. You eat decent food and work out but you still end up overweight.

'That creates tremendous challenges and frustrations, and I think that needs to be named. That needs to be recognised. Physiology is brutal. It's fundamentally unfair.'

Armed with this insight Nick found out, at fifteen, exactly what he needed to do *individually* to redress the situation and lose the weight. And he did it.

'Over the course of about seven months I lost just north of sixty pounds. It was a jaws-on-the-floor return to school from summer break.'

And for twenty years, he lived up to that teenage resolution.

Then COVID-19 happened and all his good habits disappeared. Nick's weight ballooned to 246lbs (111kg).

Proof again, if it was even needed, that knowing the path is not the same as walking the path.

Gravitational Pull

On the subject of knowing the path, Nick makes an important point. All of the books in this space are written after the finish line is crossed. The author's done it, they're on the other side, in the place where the grass is greener.

'These books can be off-putting because they present such a rosy, no-nonsense approach that seems completely straightforward.'

The other point he makes goes back to that insight he had when he was a teenager. 'The author has found the formula *that works for them*, but the reality is, everybody's formula is going to be slightly different. Are there principles that we can all pull out and lean on? Certainly. But you have to recognise that there really is no one way, no magic bullet.'

OK, so how do you bridge the gap between knowing what you need to do and actually doing it?

'Both my wife and I see therapists from time to time, just to maintain our mental health and keep everything connected,' says Nick. 'Often when you talk to a therapist, you don't walk out of there hearing anything you haven't already said yourself a million times. It's almost like the therapist mirrors it. They show things to you in a different light. Or maybe it feels more real because another person is echoing what you already know. I already knew I wanted to change ... And yet still I didn't change.'

Why?

'There is this idea that when you explore your motivation, if you go deep enough, you are going to get to this great WHY, and then, when you come face to face with it, it unlocks the infinite energy needed to go out and do this thing! I think for some people, that's probably true.'

But for others, it's not quite enough. For others, change can't come without one thing.

Trauma.

Nick's given a lot of thought to that word and cannot think of a better one.

'Trauma is anything – typically negative – that has happened that sticks with you, that changes you in some way. Now, we know that trauma can cause remarkable damage, I'm not making light of that, but it also can cause tremendous healing. To build muscle, you get sore, right? You break the muscle down and only in breaking it down does the body rebuild it a little bit stronger. So in my experience, trauma, or what we might call micro-trauma or micro-traumatic events, can make us stronger.'

For Nick, the trauma was multi-faceted. He turned thirty-eight during the lockdown, and had two children old enough now to mirror everything they saw Mum and Dad do. At the same time, he had become reluctant to look at himself in the mirror, or stand on the scales. He wasn't happy. Then came the day when he watched his wife, who had always been fit and athletic, struggle to get into her wetsuit.

'I knew that part wasn't my fault, but I still looked at myself and said, "I am part of this, we are one family."'

This was the last domino to fall. *This* is when it all started to change.

Here's his insight:

'The challenges had accumulated to the point where the inertia of inaction became less compelling than the energy to take action.'

Let's look at that sentence again. 'The inertia of inaction became less compelling than the energy to take action.'

He broke free of the gravitational pull of the burgers and the couch and moved into the gravitational pull of the broccoli and the gym.

> He broke free of the gravitational pull of the burgers and the couch and moved into the gravitational pull of the broccoli and the gym

Physiology Is Brutal

But why trauma? Why do you need something brutal to prompt change?

Because change is hard.

'Anyone who suggests that it's easy is lying to you, or else they are so far removed from the challenge that they have forgotten what it was like to see no light.'

This is a very important point, and one that those of us in the business of coaching need to acknowledge more often. Change is really, really hard.

'It's hard because, biologically, we're hunter-gatherers. We're not meant to have this nutritional abundance. In our evolutionary history we weren't always certain of when we would have access to food. Even modern hunter-gatherers – and I studied these populations – when they come across honey, they might eat five full nests in a day. They accumulate as much of that sugar as possible. But for the rest of us, that honey isn't scarce anymore. Every time we go to the shop, it's there. And our biology still calls on us to eat as much of it as we can.'

'Holding an iPhone, using a computer, driving a car; all these technological advancements have brought about lifestyle shifts that no longer demand things of you. You don't have to move anymore. Inactivity is the norm. The point is that people have to recognise that it is going to take a biologically abnormal level of energy to get the ball rolling. People need to hear that. They need to know that because if you go into this thinking it'll be easy, you will fail. The energy required to change means you have to literally go against everything your biology is built on. That, for me, is a liberating truth. You are liberated by that truth because then you don't have false expectations.'

Remember too that the trauma doesn't actually have to be your own. It can come from anywhere, and it need not even be related to healthy living. Losing someone important to you can remind you that this isn't forever.

'Traumas let you see the punch line. They show you one of several possible endings to the movie. If you don't like what you see – especially when it is related to a death – that is a force that can switch the light on in an inner room that has always been dark.'

'I believe that if your energy, your motivation, your *intention*, is not in an authentic place, you'll struggle to sustain change in the long term. When real change happens, you feel compelled to change to such an extent that you are not changing so much as *being changed*. It's as if change is being imposed on you. Again, I keep going back to that idea of gravitational pull.'

So you have to be ready for it. How can you tell if you are? Well, if these words do not resonate with you, chances are change won't stick.

'It is something that people need to feel. If you are feeling something that you can't put into words, but you have the sense that you are being compelled to take action, then you're ready, even if you're not quite sure what it is you're ready for.'

And if you don't feel ready, you can still go looking for the source of that energy.

'In my mind, it's about exploration. This is where talking can help: to a therapist, a coach, or a friend; getting them to ask the questions, "Why are you struggling to change? What do you think is going on here?" It's a process of peeling back the layers, of unpacking things.'

Nick's energy to change came from a variety of sources: his own desires; his wife's desires and his desire to see her happy;

the drive to ensure his children see his best behaviours, knowing that they adopt what they see, not what you tell them to adopt.

And when you do begin to implement change, here's his key principle: start small and win often. Don't make the mistake of starting too big. When you start big, the energy required to maintain that is just unsustainable. And when you slip up, it will seem so much more difficult to start again. You need to make a slow trade-off, so that you can build that energy and ensure that the gravitational pull builds.

Start small and win often

'During lockdown, the first thing I did was this: I started writing down what I was eating. That was it. That was the only thing I changed at first.'

This simple act forced him to confront the reality of what he was putting into his body.

'As soon as I started that, I began eating a little less in the evening, eating a bit more and a bit better during the day. By writing it down, I started to come into contact with the source of change.'

That one small initiative set the ball rolling, and it didn't take long to gain momentum.

'Writing down what I was eating prompted incremental improvements in diet, and that got me to a point where I started feeling good without really changing much of my activity. In fact, some of my activity actually went down because I was dropping my calorie intake, but that was OK. Sometimes there has to be a bit of a trade-off.'

Dancing with the Habit

To repeat: start small, win often. Also, anticipate setbacks, because setbacks are an inescapable part of all human endeavour. Ask yourself, 'What's going to get in my way?' And figure out a way round it.

'My weight sat at 238lbs [108kg] for a few months,' says Nick. 'At that stage, I'd started to work harder, my body had started to change and I looked better, but I was kind of stuck there. I wasn't happy. So, I decided to fine tune. I ate more vegetables, took out more of the refined sugars. This is not something I could have done on day one, but by then, with a little momentum behind me, these kinds of steps became possible.'

Change is a catalyst for change.

'By last December, I got down to 224lbs [102kg]. And this was with no consistent strength-training programme. It was just conscious awareness every day: be active and eat with purpose. At this point, I could stop writing things down. I needed the scaffolding to get the building up, but once it could stand on its own, I didn't need that scaffolding anymore.'

This broke Nick through the 224 plateau, and with momentum gathering, he began making body breakthroughs that he hadn't managed back in high school.

He did some research and got the nutrition tracking app he wanted.

'I nailed down calories. I nailed down carbs, fat, protein, macros, micronutrients. Everything is tracked. I weigh everything now. At the moment, I live like a body builder.

'So I'm back writing things down, in a way. I'm tracking my progress on the app to make sure I make the incremental gains to get over the finish line. And what's that? Well, I've never seen my abs in my life. Now, I know I'm going to.

'And it's no longer a chore. Now I'm using the habit for fun. I'm dancing with it.'

The key point he wants to make here is that action is the catalyst for action. The physical development/nutrition side won't be for everyone, but this is what works for Nick. And he would be the first to point out that this level of granularity wouldn't have worked for him four or five months ago. But every time he banks a win, that's a percentage increase in gravitational pull the other way.

Six key points on gaining momentum

- Be clear on what you want and why you want it

- Discover the spark to ignite that first move

- Start small

- Do anything that has a win attached to it

- Allow the momentum to build

- Anticipate obstacles and the ways to overcome them

Forcing the Habit

I've known Eamonn Sinnott, General Manager of Intel Ireland, for more than a decade now. He featured in my last book *Commit! Make Your Mind and Body Stronger and Unlock Your Full Potential*, and continues to oversee a large organisation operating in an exceptionally fast-moving and complex industry. Since 1989, the company has invested €22 billion in creating the most advanced industrial complex in Europe right here in Ireland. When you arrive into the vast Leixlip campus, there's an amazing energy everywhere. You get a real sense of the astonishing technological progress that is being made here almost every day.

Leading that drive takes huge levels of energy.

In *Commit!*, Eamonn talked about how he came to the realisation that it isn't selfish to take regular exercise, it's selfish *not* to.

'If my responsibilities make exceptional demands of me and my time, then I'm going to have to be at my best to meet those responsibilities.'

So much comes back to mindset. A fixed mindset says that my life is simply too busy for exercise. A growth mindset says, right, I need to find time for exercise, I need to think about my nutrition and hydration, I need to protect my rest and recovery time. How do I do this?

In the months that followed this epiphany, Eamonn made a series of small but significant changes to his routine in order to create the space he needed to look after himself, to boost his energy and facilitate the rapid pace at which he worked.

But it wasn't long before his punishing schedule knocked him off course. The road to hell, he points out, is paved with good intentions.

'I was at the stage where I could recite all the insights. I could tell you about the importance of a well-hydrated body, I could tell you about the importance of nutrition. I learned a lot about carbohydrates and proteins and I had an appreciation of what was right and what was wrong when it came to diet. I knew that if I went on a strict calorie regime, I could lose weight.'

'Why, then,' he asked, 'is exercise not a habit for me? When I do it, I like it, and I feel the benefits of it, so why isn't it a standard process for me?'

Eamonn is not a big fan of quotes, but Aristotle's resonated with him. 'We are what we repeatedly do. Greatness, then, is not an act, but a habit.' How do you make something, which you understand to be good, habitual?

So, as before, we went through his schedule, looking for places where exercise might be inserted. It was an old conversation, a dead-end conversation, which circled round and round: me suggesting things, and Eamonn knocking them back, until eventually I said, 'Well, can you at least do squats in the shower?'

'Squats in the shower?' he said, looking at me with scorn. What he said next is unprintable.

But that idea – doing squats in the shower – was so peculiar that it stuck with him. What was so important about squats? And why on earth would you do them in the shower? He read up about this kind of exercise, and realised how fundamental to everyday movement the squat is. Squats not only build muscle and burn calories, they help improve flexibility and aid mobility and balance. Eamonn realised that up to now, his motivation for improving his exercise had been kind of under-developed. He'd been thinking in terms of fitting into clothes, in terms of looking good. But of course there's so much more to it than that. It's about generating energy, it's about feeling good, it's about avoiding injury and preserving the quality of your life *throughout* your life.

But how do you make these movements, these little investments in quality of life, part of your everyday routine?

'My realisation', says Eamonn, 'is that everything in life is a habit: which side of the bed we sleep on, what we eat in the morning, where we park, where we shop, how we shop.'

It's true. So much of our lives happen on autopilot. Our mornings in particular tend to run along rigid habitual lines. You may know what you did yesterday morning, but can you actually remember doing it? Probably not, because it didn't take much conscious thought. It just happened because you always do it that way.

So, how do you get exercise into that framework?

Just do it. Just get up earlier and start exercising. *Force* the habit.

That's what Eamonn did, last January. And it worked. Or at least, it's working.

'It's simple things like leaving your workout gear at the end of the bed in the evening, so that the first thing you do in the morning is climb into that. That way, before you're even awake, you're into your morning routine.'

Another great insight: stop thinking about it.

'You get up on a Saturday and think, I suppose I should go for a run now. Is it raining? Looks like it's blowing a gale out there ... and my favourite gear is in the wash, and I have to get the kids to soccer or basketball by half-ten, so I probably don't have enough time. Inevitably, you end up running out of time, or talking yourself out of it. Now, as soon as I catch myself doing all that processing, I stop and just go and do it, no arguments.'

'I'm down nearly three kilos. I've missed less than 10 per cent of my planned exercise days. And I've done 100 days of walking with my wife. We haven't missed a day. It's April now, the evenings are getting brighter and we're really enjoying the arrival of spring. We can talk about it because we've seen the hedgerows in the darkest of winter days, so we're more aware of where we are and the passage of time.'

He points out too that diet is as habitual as anything else. 'The dietary stuff is hard at the beginning because you are so used to doing things like eating in front of the telly, or eating certain things at certain times of the day. Instead of creating a sense that you are depriving yourself, you create a sense of routine, of something you enjoy doing and you want to do. It's pushing through that sense of deprivation so that you imprint the pattern on yourself and it becomes something you do without even thinking about it.'

Hydration was relatively easy. He simply got into the habit of filling his two-litre bottle every morning, and keeping it with him throughout the day, though it's usually empty by noon.

'I'm on a great trajectory and bringing my wife and kids with me. That's the kind of culture that we have built up almost accidently in the house now. Exercise is a life lesson rather than a vanity project.'

Eamonn found a tipping point, where that huge effort of will was no longer necessary, and the regime, the lifestyle, became ordinary.

'It became a habit, a habit you do without even thinking. Then you start to enjoy it more and you think, maybe I can go a little bit faster, maybe a little further. The big question, in a post-pandemic world, is whether or not these habits will withstand the return of executive travel and office pressures. The way I think about it is, well, am I going to brush my teeth every day when I travel?'

In Summary

- You need to customise your approach to health and wellbeing. Find a way to stack up positive daily habits.
- Start small and win often.
- Build the momentum until positive actions become habitual.
- Anticipate obstacles before you hit them.

CHAPTER 6:

NO EGO

'More the Knowledge, Lesser the Ego' – Einstein

I talked earlier about playing Gaelic football in college. One time, we were playing local rivals St Mary's at home, in a game we should have won. But we didn't. They beat us badly in our own backyard. At the time, we had great ambitions to win the Sigerson Cup, which is the senior intervarsity Gaelic football competition. Losing at home to St Mary's, however, showed us just how unrealistic that ambition was. It might only have been a league loss, but it seemed bigger. And everyone felt it. I vividly remember coming back into the changing rooms after the final whistle. Everyone was slumped on the benches, panting and soaked with sweat. There was a growing pile of jerseys in the middle of the floor, steam rising gently from it. Nobody spoke. There was nothing to say. Next thing, our coach Dessie Ryan walked in. Dessie is a legend of the game, and remains, at seventy-seven years of age, one of the fittest men I know. He came into the changing room, but there was no rousing speech, and no recriminations either. He sat down among us, just as demoralised, just as frustrated, just as disappointed. Nobody got up, nobody headed to the showers.

Eventually, he spoke. In a very calm, unemotional voice, he said, 'Gentlemen, I feel very angry about what just happened out there. We let ourselves down. I let you down. Our strategy was wrong, the tactical decisions we made were wrong. Our preparation was wrong and I take full responsibility for that.'

Just as he said this, the winning team began trooping in from the pitch. They were shouting and laughing, and as they passed our door, they began banging on it with their fists. Dessie fell silent and the door shuddered and shook with the violence of the hammering. It went on and on. Three minutes, four minutes. You couldn't hear yourself think. Eventually, when they were all in their own changing room, they started singing. The usual stuff: *'Championes, championes, olé olé olé ...'* and we could hear them lacing our name into their victory chants. The minute their door closed and the noise subsided a little, Dessie sat up straight. His whole demeanour changed. He no longer looked beaten.

'When we win the Sigerson,' he said, 'their silence will be our song.'

And he grabbed his bag and left the room.

Dessie was old school. Teak tough. And like I say, fitter than most men half his age.

'When we win the Sigerson, their silence will be our song'

A few years back, I went to Tullamore to watch him compete in the Irish Masters athletics championships. He was seventy-three at the time, and I could not believe how fast he was. The following night, I went out with my brother Paul to see if we could get the same times he got in the 200 metres and 400 metres. Neither of us could.

Dessie played football in Tyrone in the late fifties, then emigrated to New York where he became a fireman with the sixteenth Battalion, fifth division in Harlem. That's where he cut his teeth as a leader. He also played football for New York, and won National League titles with the exiles in 1964 and 1967. To this day, he's the highest-scoring player they ever had. He came home in the seventies, and went on to open a pub – Ryan's Bar – in Ballyronan, Co. Derry. He started coaching Queen's in 1990, a few years before I got there, and managed to win the Sigerson in his first season in charge.

Dessie may have been old school, but his methods were nothing like those of his contemporaries. He never ranted, never threw things, never spoke in clichés. Everything he said was carefully thought out.

The crucial difference between Dessie and the ordinary, run-of-the-mill coach, however, was this: he was prepared to be vulnerable in front of those he led. When we lost that game, he sat among us, as dejected as we were. He let us see him hurting. This wasn't old-school leadership, where the general has to look invincible in front of his troops.

The second thing that made him different was this: he took full responsibility for the failure. As our leader, he saw where he had gone wrong and admitted it in front of us. He explained how he'd screwed up. That kind of honesty is rare. And it's powerful. It opened us up, it created fertile ground where he could sow a little hope. Because right at the end, he sat up straight, lifted his head – completely transforming his stature – and told us that their silence would be our song. We might have felt that our Sigerson ambitions were dead in the water, but he didn't. He believed we could come back from this. We saw someone hurting just as much as we were, but his belief was unwavering.

Was there also a bit of theatre at work here? Sure there was. Dessie used every trick in the book to motivate his teams, but that kind of thing won't work if the leader has no credibility. Here was a leader who wasn't afraid to fail, wasn't afraid to look weak in front of his people, and wasn't afraid to take responsibility for his actions.

Did it work? Did we go on to win the Sigerson that year? We did, yes, but I wouldn't pretend that it was all down to that one little episode. Our victory was built on many things, but belief was one of them, and that belief sparked to life in the changing room after that loss.

Ego Is the Enemy

Authentic leadership is about showing your team when you're vulnerable. It's being honest when you're unsure. Last year, in our organisation, we set ourselves some pretty ambitious targets. I told the team I wasn't certain that we were going to hit those numbers, but I was 100 per cent sure that the team we had gave us the best chance of doing it. You tell a team you're absolutely certain you're going to win and they'll know you're bluffing. Giving them certainties at a time when there are no certainties communicates fear and insecurity. Put yourself out there. Show them you're human and you'll get more respect. People can empathise with vulnerability because they see something of themselves in it. It's much harder to connect with someone who never shows weakness, who never allows their humanity to be seen. I call that plastic leadership, and it's not leadership at all.

Ego is the enemy. The more removed a leader is from their people, the more difficult it will be to lead them. Cees Hart, CEO of the Carlsberg Group, gave up his twentieth-floor corner office two months after taking up the job. Instead, he took an empty desk in an open-plan office on a lower floor. 'If I don't meet people,' he said, 'I won't get to know what they think. And if I don't have a finger on the pulse of the organisation, I can't lead effectively.'[1]

Some of the most impressive leaders I've ever met don't have offices at all, let alone a corner office with panelled walls and panoramic views. Pádraig Ó Céidigh built a €100 million airline by staying among his people all the time. The closest he came to having a corner office was when Aer Arann was first establishing itself; he shared a desk in a Portakabin in Dublin Airport.

The truth is that the leader serves those they lead, not the other way round. No one individual drives an organisation forward. Your team does that. If you can't give them what they need to facilitate that progress, you fail. So if you distance yourself from those you lead, you'll end up in a bubble – a nice bubble with panelled walls and a great view – but a bubble nonetheless, and no one can lead from a bubble.

Being ego-led also leaves you vulnerable. If you're hung up on your status, you're going to end up surrounded by sycophants and yes-people. You'll be insecure and easy to manipulate. And that insecurity clouds your vision. If you're primarily focused on preserving your own position, at the very least you're going to miss things. At worst, you'll drive the whole organisation off the road.

> If you're hung up on your status, you're going to end up surrounded by sycophants and yes-people

We live in a time of constant flux. To lead, you need continual self-development, continual learning. The ego-led leader won't confront gaps in their skill sets; it's too painful for them to face the awful truth, which is that they don't know everything.

Tim O'Connor is a former chief of staff to the President of Ireland and a former consul general of Ireland in New York. Most of his career in the Department of Foreign Affairs was spent working on the Northern Ireland Peace Process. I first met Tim at Seamus Mallon's funeral, where, as I mentioned earlier, he gave a wonderful eulogy for his friend. Afterwards, I asked if he'd meet me for coffee. I'm always on the lookout for people I can learn from, people with rich experience and a shared drive to realise their potential and that of everyone else. Tim is over seventy now, and retired, but a man like that never really retires. Any time I meet him for coffee, he's always deeply involved in some new project.

'I am always trying to learn,' he says. 'I've learned so much even since I retired. I'm always listening and watching out for new perspectives. I am not just sitting there like a Buddha, dispensing and transmitting. Learning is a key part of leadership. There's a necessary humility about it. It's understanding that you don't have all the answers, and that somebody in the room might have something that you don't have.'

These days, I can tell as soon as I walk into the room how coachable the CEO is. I can tell before I even walk into the room. Just this week I had a coaching session with the CEO of a global corporation. Two weeks ago, he sent in his report for the year to date, setting out how he had progressed on the goals he had set himself, goals which took in both his personal and his professional life, and which covered everything from energy management and wellbeing to financial health. This is someone who knows that he does not have all the answers; he knows that he needs the right people around him to enable his leadership. And alongside that he has a fierce, purpose-driven determination to achieve. Leaders who are humble, hungry to learn and grounded in reality are a joy to coach.

Level 5 Leaders

The aforementioned Pádraig Ó Céidigh is an example of what author Jim Collins would call a Level 5 leader: 'an individual who blends extreme personal humility with intense professional will'.[2]

In his seminal work *Good to Great,* Collins says: 'Level 5 leaders channel their ego needs away from themselves and into the larger goal of building a great company. It's not that Level 5 leaders have no ego or self-interest. Indeed, they are incredibly ambitious – but their ambition is first and foremost for the institution, not themselves.'[3]

I think Collins captures that unique mix that all great leaders have. Alongside the humility, there is a fierce determination to succeed. Dessie Ryan might have been able to share in our dejection, he might have been ready to admit responsibility for our failure, but his eyes were firmly fixed on that trophy. His training sessions were legendary – sometimes running for three or four hours. And his commitment to winning was unwavering.

When Jim Collins and the research group he led set out to find out how good companies became great, he didn't look at leadership, not initially. He wanted to avoid simplistic 'credit the leader' or 'blame the leader' thinking, and really get to the heart of what it was that made great companies great. What he discovered, however, was that he couldn't explain the outperformance of certain companies, and the underperformance of others, without looking at their leadership.

'The good-to-great executives were all cut from the same cloth [#] ... It didn't matter when the transition took place or how big the company. All the good-to-great companies had Level 5 leadership at the time of transition.'[4]

Moreover, the absence of Level 5 leadership showed up consistently in companies that failed to make the grade.

It's interesting, too, to look at a list of the top-twenty Fortune 500 companies. Apart from perhaps Warren Buffet and Apple's Tim Cook, none of their leaders are household names.

While the media like to focus on the big, brash, larger-than-life leaders, most of the successful ones are unassuming people who dodge the limelight.

Collective Leadership

Rory Best is another Level 5 leader. It's no coincidence that the Irish rugby team beat so many of the world's biggest teams under his captaincy. Rory is an Armagh man like me, and, like me, he grew up on a farm. In that environment, no one gets a free pass. There's a great deal of hard work to be done, and everyone in the family is expected to pull their weight. That kind of thing builds character like nothing else.

He says, 'My career has always been about the collective being stronger than the individual. I wasn't blessed with out-rageous individual talent. My strengths lie in my knowledge and reading of the game. I wasn't somebody who said, "Give me the ball and I'll make things happen." I knew that if I did my job right, I could create momentum and space for those around me to do their thing. That's why ego was never a mas-sive issue.'

When I asked Rory what the hardest thing about becoming captain of Ireland was, he surprised me by saying that it was simply being himself.

'First of all there's the magnitude of it, and the euphoria at being asked to be captain. The pride is enormous. But as the first camp drew nearer, it started to dawn on me. What am I going to do? How am I going to *be*? I was among some of the best players in the world, and I was thinking about the shoes

I'd just stepped into. I almost felt pressured into doing it the way Paulie (Paul O'Connell) did it or Brian (O'Driscoll) did it. They were two of the captains I played under. It's really hard to step back and say, "That's *them*, that's how *they* were. Yes, there are always things you can learn from great captains, but you can't try to do what they did."'

If Rory had acted like Brian or like Paul, if he had attempted to do exactly as they had done, it would have been inauthentic; it would have communicated uncertainty and insecurity to the team. The best way, the only way, forward was to find a way to lead that was true to who he was.

'I realised I couldn't make it about me, about stamping my authority on the team, because that's just not who I am. Also I had two guys who captained their provinces – Johnny Sexton and Pete O'Mahony. It would have been madness to exclude them or try to speak over them. And I knew too that when Paulie was captain, if one of those two said something, I listened. Everyone listened. So why make the job harder for myself? I realised that I could divide the captaincy workload up by letting the people around me inspire me.'

'I needed to remember too, that I was a player on the team. As captain, you need to motivate, guide and make the right decisions, but it's not that easy to inspire yourself, so it was important to let people like Johnny and Pete and Keith Earls speak, because more often than not, something they might say would strike a chord with me as a player.'

> 'I realised that I could divide the captaincy workload up by letting the people around me inspire me'

He explains that his captaincy was also about leading by example.

'If I can be motivated, and at the right emotional pitch, that is going to help the group.'

In the run-up to the 2019 World Cup, A TV company proposed a fly-on-the-wall documentary, which would feature Ireland's progress at the tournament. At first, Rory was in favour of the idea. He was thinking of his own children, who were young at the time. Participating in a World Cup is a great honour for any player, and having a film record of it would be something he could show them in years to come.

'It was Johnny who made the point – and this is ultimately the reason we didn't do it – that when you introduce a camera in the corner of the room, suddenly people start talking absolute nonsense. The people you don't want speaking suddenly start speaking, and the right people see the camera and clam up. When I say "the right people", that could be anyone – as long as they're genuine, as long as they say something they truly believe in. Keith Earls was a great example of that. He didn't speak often, but when he did, you knew that it meant something to him.'

It's true, though. A camera is an excellent device for ego-detection. The best leader is the one who finds themselves in a leadership position because that's the best place to make things happen. The worst leader is the one who seeks a leadership position because it's cool.

Rory says, 'One big thing I learned under Joe Schmidt was this: I had always felt that as captain, you needed to have the last word. I got it into my head that if you didn't have the last word that, well, maybe people would think you weren't in charge and all this sort of nonsense. Joe said to me quite early on, "Look Rory, you don't need to be last person to speak." What you don't realise is that when you speak after someone, you undermine them a little bit. So let them talk, let them have their say, even if you might not agree entirely with what they're saying.'

I vividly remember Rory at half-time in the changing rooms in Soldier Field in Chicago, before he led the Irish team out to complete what they had started in the first half and defeat the All Blacks for the first time. He brought the team together into a huddle in the centre of the room to talk about the coming forty minutes. He never raised his voice, he never thumped the table, he didn't talk about the eye of history or any of that stuff. He talked calmly about the job that lay before them, about each man fulfilling his role, about sticking to the basics and winning the moments that mattered. There was a contagious calmness about him.

Rory returns again to that original point. As a leader, you don't have to take the world on your shoulders. By spreading the burden around, you are demonstrating trust in those you captain, you're empowering those you lead to lead themselves. This is transformative leadership at its best.

'I might say to Johnny or Pete on the Thursday ahead of a big game, "Johnny, you run the session, I don't intend to say a thing all day." Joe gave me the comfort to do that, and it was an approach I took with me back to Ulster, and found that it was an incredibly empowering tool.'

I sometimes hear people complain about the loneliness of leadership. This, I believe, is a red flag. Feeling isolated, feeling alone, is often an ego issue. It is evidence that the leader is afraid to reach out, afraid to be seen as vulnerable, fallible, human. The idea of the lone wolf might seem romantic, but in nature, lone wolves fare far worse than those in packs. In fact, when a wolf loses its pack for whatever reason, its first priority is to find a new one.[5]

Bernard Byrne, former CEO of AIB, acknowledges that the leader can end up more isolated and that, when times are tough, the good leader is always careful about protecting their team.

'But you are not totally isolated,' he says. 'Far from it. You have a board, you have a chairman. Really, though, I think that most people who survive in leadership are those who make sure that they have people to talk to.'

In Summary

- Showing vulnerability ultimately gives you power.
- Great leaders never isolate themselves. Stay among your people.
- Level 5 leaders are far more ambitious for their team and their organisation than for themselves.
- Strive to harness the leadership skills of *everyone* in the organisation.

CHAPTER 7:

EMPATHY

EQ Is More Important Than IQ

There's been so much said and written about emotional intelligence that the definition is sometimes lost. There's two parts to it. Being emotionally intelligent means being able to understand and manage your own emotions *and* being able to recognise, understand and influence the emotions of others. Intelligence – IQ – is great, it's vital for effective leadership, but any leader is continually confronted by the jumbled emotions of all the people they lead. If they lack the skills to read, understand and respond to these emotions, all of the smarts in the world won't help.

I want to return again to Shackleton, stranded with his crew, watching *Endurance* being consumed by the ice.

> Any leader is continually confronted by the jumbled emotions of all the people they lead

It was October 1915. They were over a thousand miles from the nearest human settlement, and there was no hope of rescue. Even the most hardened of the polar veterans among them feared for their survival. How much greater those fears would have been if they had known that they were destined to spend the next six months on the ice.

Standing there that day Shackleton addressed the crew. 'We're in a spot,' he said, 'but we're going to get out of it. Before I tell you what the plan is, I want to thank you for the way you've carried on. No men ever did better.'[1]

The plan, at the time, was to strike out across the ice for Paulet Island, 350 miles away. There, there would be supplies and shelter. In the meantime, the only option was to camp out on the ice itself.

That first night, Shackleton didn't go to bed, but spent the hours of darkness patrolling the lines of tents. Twice, he gave the alarm when the ice began to break up and the men were forced to move to what they hoped would be safer ground. The second time, they were so tired, they didn't bother putting the tents back up but bedded down on the ice. At dawn, Shackleton, together with Frank Wild and another early riser, Frank Hurley, went from one huddle of sleepers to another handing out hot milk.[2]

Morale rose as the men prepared to depart, but Shackleton shattered the mood when he called them together and told them that they could not carry everything.

'Get rid of all but two pounds of your personal things.'[3]

He knew how difficult it would be for the men to work out which cherished personal things to abandon, so he immediately dug in his pocket and pulled out a handful of gold sovereigns. He took his watch from the other pocket and threw the lot into the snow. The only exception he made was not for himself, but for the meteorologist, Leonard Hussey, who played the banjo. Shackleton understood that music would have an important role in overcoming the mental challenges that lay ahead, and so Leonard kept his banjo.

In the months that followed, they hauled supplies – which included three substantial boats – across treacherous floes, camping out on the ice for weeks on end. It was hell: backbreaking labour in freezing conditions and on starvation rations. Morale flagged and tempers flared.

But Shackleton had made it his business to know his men well. He grouped them into tents according to their temperaments and moved them frequently to prevent cliques forming. He got to know all of their interests, and would speak to them individually about the things they were most passionate about. The difficult men, those who had trouble getting on with anyone, slept in his tent.

As winter came on, the nights became longer, the weather deteriorated and rations dwindled to almost nothing. One by one, they were forced to kill and eat the dogs. There were so many brushes with death that they lost count. To the men, who called Shackleton 'Canny Jack', it looked as though he was riding his luck. The reality was far more mundane. Shackleton slept less than any of them, spending most of his time pacing in his tent, imagining obstacles to come and trying to figure out a way around them. That was how he stayed lucky.

Land was sighted in March of 1916: Mount Percy on Join-ville Island. The men were delirious with excitement. Land, actual land, and within striking distance. But when Shackle-ton climbed down from the lookout tower they had built, he shook his head and told them that crossing the thinning ice which separated them from the island was too dangerous. He would not risk it. These men had drifted aimlessly in the floe for 2,000 miles. When they heard Shackleton's decision, they were devastated – but not one of them questioned him.

'His buoyancy and determination infected his men – even the most dispirited. He constantly cajoled, joked, argued, prod-ded, pushed and led. He shared their rations, hardships, games and songs. He was one of them, yet always their leader.'[5]

The physical challenges these men overcame were extraor-dinary. But the mental challenges? They were off the scale. These were men with all kinds of temperaments and abilities and backgrounds and human failings. But each one responded to something in Shackleton. They could see his ability and intelligence – they were clear – but clearer still was the fact that all of that ability and intelligence was being used to do one thing, and one thing only. Keep them alive.

Each man knew that Shackleton cared about them, and that worked magic in their minds.

Emotional Intelligence

Dr Mary Collins defines three key competencies that feed into emotional intelligence: optimism, self-control and empathy.

'The good news for leaders is they can all be developed.

They're like a muscle. You can develop optimism, you can develop self-control and you can develop empathy.'

We talked about self-control and optimism earlier. Right now, I want to focus on the third element. Empathy.

Empathy, Mary says, can sometimes be seen as a bit fluffy, a bit touchy-feely.

It's not.

'Empathy is your key business-development lever, your key business-relationship driver. Empathy is about understanding someone else's framework, it's about tuning into where somebody is at, so that the other person feels heard, feels listened to, feels understood.'

That last part is important. It's not enough to tune into someone else's wavelength. They've got to *know* that you're tuned in, that you *get it*.

> It's not enough to tune into someone else's wavelength. They've got to *know* that you're tuned in, that you *get it*

Everyone is different. We face different challenges, we care about different things, we favour different ways of communicating. Different things excite us and scare us and bore us.

You've got to know each one of your people well in order to successfully empathise.

'The pillar of empathy is active listening,' says Mary. 'Creating the space for your people to really understand and connect with what's going on with them, that's empathy.'

Much of Mary's research has explored the things that differentiate the various age cohorts in the workplace, from centennials and millennials up to baby boomers.

'The first formal study of centennials in the US was completed at the end of last year,' she says. 'This surveyed over 5,000 18–24-year-olds. What I thought was fascinating was that the top two things they're looking for at work were number one, supportive leadership, and number two, positive relationships.'

Another study found that this generation also reports the highest levels of loneliness.[6]

'Typically,' says Mary, 'we think loneliness as an issue for older people, but workplace loneliness is on the rise.'

When you translate that back into our remote-working, post-COVID world, you'll see just how much more difficult supportive leadership becomes.

'It's never been more important to connect with your people. We talk about the CEO as the Chief Empathy Officer, and that's where your emotional intelligence comes in. A lot of my work these days centres on how you can create social connection in a virtual world, how you can have a people-focused culture in a virtual world.'

Keeping Channels Open

Multiple surveys in the aftermath of successive COVID lockdowns found that a large proportion of the workforce was thinking about changing jobs. Microsoft found that 41 per cent of the global workforce is 'likely to consider leaving their current employer within the next year'.[7]

'A lot of that', says Mary, 'is down to the fact that people don't have that connection or loyalty to the employer if they are home-working. That emphasises the need to amplify your communication, your connection. Empathy becomes more important than ever.'

In a remote-working world, communications tend to become formal. You don't reach out to a colleague unless you need something. There's no catching someone's eye across the office and nodding hello, no talking about the weekend, there are no water-cooler conversations, no falling into step with somebody when you're going to lunch. And there's a tendency, too, to default to video calls, which don't suit everyone, and which often generate significant levels of stress.

If the informality has been lost from your communications, reintroduce it. Set aside ten or fifteen minutes on the Monday-morning call to talk about your weekend, to catch up on each other's news. For younger people in particular, the workplace is a vital source of social connection. If that connection is disrupted, they have less reason to stay with you.

Remember too that empathy, like resilience, can be taught; it's not a case of you either have it or you don't.

Mary Collins talks about a recent experience coaching a senior partner in a law firm.

'We did some profiling and he scored really low on empathy. So he put a reminder in his calendar. *Every Monday morning, ask the team how their weekend went.* I kid you not. He actually needed those prompts. But it began to bear fruit almost immediately. He reported that his team responded really positively to this, and that he was enjoying these new interactions himself. They had built into a new habit.'

She's quick to point out that this has to be done in an authentic way. If it becomes a box-ticking exercise, no one's going to buy it. In this case, however, the manager's genuine desire to connect made the initiative ring true.

The Inspirational Gardener

My friend and colleague Eugene Conlon has extensive experience in HR and change management. He agrees that while it's important for a leader to be smart, being smart is no longer enough – if it ever was.

'In the world we live in today, people want to feel inspired. They want to see that what they're doing contributes to their quality of life and to the lives of other people.'

Inspiration, he says, isn't something you get from a fiery speech. Hiring a motivational speaker to give the troops their annual shot of inspiration is about the most uninspiring thing you can do. OK, some people may feel fired up afterwards, but that's just a feeling and feelings come and go.

Real inspiration emerges from relationships based on (and here's that word again) trust. Eugene believes that trust rests on three pillars:

Credibility: Is what this person says credible? Do their words and actions rhyme?

Capability: The intelligence bit. Have they demonstrated an ability to make sound decisions?

Intimacy: Do I feel a bond with this individual?

This is how Eugene describes feeling inspired: 'It's that sense that I can trust this person. It's seeing them as human and knowing that they see me as human. They may not be the best speaker in the world but they have an interest in ensuring that I'm successful as an employee and that I like working here.'

I couldn't agree more.

The best analogy I can think of is that of a gardener. They don't go into the tomatoes in the greenhouse and shout, 'Hurry up! What's keeping you? Grow faster!' The gardener knows that you have to get the environment right. You need the right amount of light and water. The soil has to be appropriate to what you're trying to grow. You may need to bring in compost or fertiliser. You'll need to remove weeds. The gardener knows that some young plants need extra support in the early days: that little bamboo cane a young tree relies upon to set it growing straight and true. The gardener knows, too, that for the garden to thrive, they must tend to it every day. Stopping in at the end of the month to check on things won't work. It's a process of continual nurturing.

You need to celebrate the successes of your team. Let them know that you recognise their victories and the effort that went into them. Knowing that you're appreciated, that what you've done makes a difference, there's no more powerful motivator.

In any customer-facing operation, the customer will always be king, but in the best, most forward-thinking organisations that I've dealt with, the employee is elevated to that same position.

In the summer of 2019, recruitment company Glassdoor brought together two large data sets: their own employee ratings and ratings from the American Customer Satisfaction Index. They wanted to see if there was any correlation between high employee satisfaction and high customer satisfaction. The research spanned 293 large employers across thirteen industries.

'Our answer was clear: there is a strong statistical link between employee wellbeing reported on Glassdoor and customer satisfaction among a large sample of some of the largest companies today. A happier workforce is clearly associated with companies' ability to deliver better customer satisfaction – particularly in industries with the closest contact between workers and customers, including retail, tourism, restaurants, health care and financial services.'[8]

The conclusion the researchers reached is that if you want to build a customer-first strategy seek high employee morale first.

In Summary

- Being emotionally intelligent means being able to understand and manage your own emotions and being able to recognise, understand and influence the emotions of others.

- Even the teak-tough adventurer Ernest Shackleton was emotionally intelligent. What about you? Do you have the courage and skill to really get to know your team?

- Three key competencies feed into emotional intelligence: optimism, self-control and empathy. ALL can be developed.

- Strive to forge close connections – especially in an increasingly remote world.

- Trust rests on three pillars: credibility, capability and intimacy.

SECTION II –
LEADING OTHERS

CHAPTER 8:

PREPARATION

Devil's Chasm

Ten years ago, I was in Arizona with Intel. We had been asked to put together a three-day programme designed to help participants build resilience into their lives. This was one of the biggest projects our company had ever been involved in, and I spent about three months working on it.

On the Thursday afternoon Brian McCarson, one of their senior engineers, asked me if I'd be interested in going on a hiking trip that weekend, to a place in the remote Sierra Ancha wilderness called the Devil's Chasm. It had been occupied by the Salado people until around 1200 AD. Brian told me that there was a spectacular ancient ruin deep in the wilderness, at the end of a three-and-a-half-hour hike.

I grew up on the side of a mountain – Slieve Gullion in

Armagh – and the idea of a long hike, especially in wild, unfamiliar terrain, really appealed to me. I hadn't expected to go hiking, so I didn't have any gear with me, but I figured I could pick up what I needed in town.

Brian told me that the start of the trail lay about a half-day's car journey into the mountains. In the canteen that Thursday, he said, 'This is very difficult terrain. Dry, rocky, steep. It's going to be hot as hell. We're going to have to get an early start. You sure you're up for this?'

'Sure,' I said, 'I'll give it a shot.'

On the Friday, I found an outdoor store and ran around it, buying boots and other bits and pieces that might come in handy on the hike, and on the Saturday morning, I was standing outside the door of the hotel at 5.30 a.m. when Brian pulled up in the jeep. Looking out at the terrain passing by as we drove through the mountains, I began to relish the adventure ahead.

But when I opened the door of the air-conditioned SUV five hours later, it was like opening the door of an oven. This was Arizona heat; so dry you could feel it in the back of your throat.

The going was easy enough at the beginning; we followed the course of a river for several hundred yards. Then these huge red cliff walls reared up on either side and began to close in on us. The going became much tougher.

It was very rocky underfoot, with seams of a kind of yielding red clay that your feet would sink into. No trees, or at least very few trees, just these prickly, cactus-type plants like those I had seen in cowboy movies as a kid.

Then there were the snakes.

We'd hardly been walking more than half an hour when I heard it. A rattle. Slightly ahead of me on the path. I froze, staring into the undergrowth.

'What was that?' I said, knowing the answer.

'Rattlesnake,' said Brian, striding on ahead.

I edged around the patch of undergrowth that had rattled and kept going, taking considerably more care about where I put my feet. Less than 30 metres further on, there was another rattle, this time from just behind me. Instinctively, I skipped ahead and turned around. Again, there was no sign of anything.

And that quickly became the pattern. There seemed to be snakes everywhere, but the worst of it, the most unnerving thing, was that I couldn't actually see them. I could only hear them.

'Don't stand on them,' said Brian.

As we went on, even that looked like a tall order, because there was no clear path; my feet kept disappearing into prickly green undergrowth, or into that dry red clay. I never had any idea what was there, and all the time, the rattles were sounding off all around us.

Brian had calculated that this was a seven-hour round trip, but that assumed that we'd be moving quite quickly. A couple of things, however, started to slow us down. First, there was the terrain. Very mountainous, very varied. We had to climb over huge boulders that had fallen from the towering red cliffs overhead, then make our way up steep slopes with our feet sliding on loose stones.

Then there was the heat. The sun was high and there was no shelter from it. It beat down on us continually. We were both sweating profusely.

We had been following a map, but after a while we started coming upon these small piles of red stones. We guessed that these were navigational points, leading the way to our destination, so after meeting four or five of these every 500 metres or so, we decided to abandon the map and follow them instead.

What happened next was predictable. We walked for an hour without seeing another of those little piles of stones.

At this stage, we started to get a bit fearful. We were very clearly lost, and time was against us. We had food and water for seven hours, no more. If we remained lost, there would be a very real risk of not getting back before the light failed, which would leave us stranded deep in the wilderness without any water. This far from civilisation, there was neither a mobile nor a GPS signal.

We didn't know whether to go left, right, forward, back ... but nor did we want to abandon the trek and give up the idea of actually getting there. Now, sitting here, **We were very clearly lost, and time was against us** writing this, the obvious course of action would have been to go back and pick up on the last navigational point we had seen, but we weren't smart enough to do that. Instead, we kept going; lost, running out of water, surrounded by snakes and with darkness on the way.

The next disaster: Brian, who was walking ahead of me, pushed through a bush and a branch whipped backwards and struck me in the left eye, which immediately filled with blood and water. I couldn't open it for the rest of the day.

Then, an hour and a half after seeing the last navigational point, we rounded a corner and there was another of those little piles of red stones. At that point, however, Brian had had enough. We'd run out of food and water and he couldn't go on. We knew we were less than an hour away from Devil's Chasm, so once I was sure he was comfortable, I pushed on.

I ran when I could, I climbed when I had to, until I eventually came to the base of the ruins. And yes, they were interesting – a series of stone houses built into the side of a cliff. But as I stood there, panting, sweating, thirsty, hungry, staring up at these things, I had to ask myself, had they been worth it? Really?

I didn't hang around. I took some pictures, then turned back.

It took ages to find Brian, and when I did, we could both see that lack of water was going to be a problem. When we could stand it no longer, we strained some river water through a T-shirt – something one of us remembered from some TV programme. We each took a small drink and, moving painstakingly slowly, we made it back down to the car just as night was falling.

One of the many ironies here is that the resilience programme we'd designed for the client – the whole reason we were in Arizona – had been minutely planned. I'd put three months into building the programme and stress-testing every element of it, to make sure that each second was absolutely as good as it could possibly be – making sure there were no weak links, no surprises, nothing that wouldn't exceed the expectations of our client.

And then, that same weekend, off I go on one of the stupidest, most ill-advised, unplanned adventures of my career. We didn't bring enough food, enough water, we didn't have the right equipment, didn't have enough respect for the terrain, the climate, the snakes even. We risked so much for a goal that was more or less meaningless. Talking about it with Brian afterwards, he agreed that though he had put in more planning than I had, we had made some pretty poor decisions along the way.

Don't get me wrong. It's not that I'm against going off-piste – far from it. I'm hardwired to seek adventure, to go looking for something new and different, but if you're going to do that, you can't do it blind. You *must* prepare. Consciously or unconsciously, I had decided that I was too tough to use a compass, too special to bring enough water. The bottom line here is that being innovative doesn't absolve you of the need to plan.

> Being innovative doesn't absolve you of the need to plan

We were lucky it wasn't more serious, we were lucky one of us didn't fall or get bitten, or pass out from dehydration. We were utterly complacent and nearly paid the price. If there was ever a cautionary tale, an object lesson in how to go about things the wrong way, this was it.

Ask yourself if you're making any of these mistakes on your leadership journey. Have you planned ahead? Do you have contingencies in place for the obstacles and setbacks that you will inevitably encounter? Do you have the skills and resources necessary to achieve the goals you've set? Does your team wander off the beaten path? Is your training everything it needs to be to allow you to execute the task effectively? Most importantly of all, is your goal the right one? Is it meaningful? Does it resonate with your values and those of the organisation?

Preparation Is Nine-tenths of the Law

There's the wrong way to go about things, and then there's the right way. On 5 November 2016 in Soldier Field in Chicago, the Irish Rugby team made history by beating the mighty All Blacks for the first time, on a score line of 40–29. It was an incredible performance, one that catapulted that team to the top of the international rankings and made us the best international rugby team in the world. As a high-performance coach with that squad, I was privileged to observe how a leader of Joe Schmidt's calibre went about preparing for a challenge of that magnitude.

I think the most telling thing about Joe wasn't what he did before the game, but what he did afterwards. On the flight home, Joe was sitting just behind me, and while everyone else was sleeping or watching movies, Joe had his laptop open and spent the first half of the flight analysing the game they had just won. But the second half of the flight? He spent that preparing for the second game of that autumn series. We all remember that day in Soldier Field, but who remembers who we played seven days later? Canada. A wonderful country, but not really a power in world rugby.

When Ireland won the New Zealand game, Joe celebrated with the team, but those celebrations didn't go on and on, despite the historic nature of the victory. When the plane landed in Dublin, he went straight to Carton House, which was the squad base for the autumn internationals. We had a second team ready to go for the Canada match, and Joe, who hadn't slept, talked to them with the same energy, focus, drive and basic excellence as he had spoken with before the All Blacks game.

This was an object lesson in how great leaders deliver great performances.

They prepare.

Joe is probably one of the best communicators I've ever seen – I'm going to talk about that a little later on. His preparation for meetings was second to none, better than anybody I've ever met in business or sport, in any leadership crucible.

During that 2018/19 period, when Ireland was the greatest team in the world, every man on that pitch knew exactly what his job was. Not only that, but, critically, they knew exactly *why* they were doing what they were doing. This was the secret ingredient. The thorough understanding of how each move fitted into the whole was what supercharged that team.

Rory Best puts it like this: 'I think ultimately it wasn't about Joe just telling us what to do, saying 'here is the mechanism'. It was all about *why* we were doing it that way. Each of us understood our role. Other teams would copy Joe's plays but they could not pull them off. You know why? The individual players didn't understand their roles within that play.'

Rory explains that the key to one of Joe's set pieces might not actually be the guy catching the ball, or the guy giving the pass, or the guy coming through the gap to receive the ball. It might actually be the guy in the ruck. He understands that he cleans out, then stands up and turns his back so that the opposition player has to deviate to go round him, and that gives the additional fraction of a second needed to open a half-gap to facilitate the break.

'So we didn't just know the play, we knew our roles within it. We knew just how important those roles were. That was the bit we did better than everyone else, that was the level of preparation he brought to the game.'

Ahead of any major international, Joe might analyse upwards of forty hours of video. He would dissect each of Ireland's six preceding games with that opposition, minutely examining set pieces and open play, looking for patterns in the data, looking for strengths and probing for weaknesses. Suppose we were playing England. He would also scrutinise England's games against everyone else they had played that season and the previous season. Then, in front of the team on the Sunday night, he could show specific pieces of footage and say, 'I spotted a gap here, so this is the play that's going to work just before half-time,' or 'This is what we're going to do off the base of the scrum.'

If you're sitting there, listening to your coach talk in detail about each opposition player and the characteristics of his game, if you see just how much work he's put into developing a strategy, what happens? You sit up. You begin to believe. You begin to see how it will work. And then, when you do what he tells you and it actually works, that belief, that confidence reaches a whole new level.

In Twickenham on a grand-slam weekend, when you see a play coming off that you've watched the team rehearse again and again over the previous eight weeks – is there a more powerful measure of the quality of the preparation that led to that exquisite moment?

That level of preparation generated huge confidence in the team. You could see it in the way they moved, the way they talked, the way they acted when they fell behind. There was no panic because there was a plan in place, a meticulously detailed plan, and the plan was understood by everyone on the pitch.

All confidence, all belief, is built on preparation.

Rory says, 'Joe was as likely to praise Tadhg Furlong for hitting four rucks in a row to get the ball to Jacob [Stockdale] so he could eventually score his try in

All confidence, all belief, is built on preparation

the corner. And that gave you confidence because, do you know what? The unseen stuff wasn't unseen anymore.'

Putting in that kind of work – forty hours of video analysis – takes astonishing levels of energy and drive. You can't just decide, right, that's what I'll do, I'll match Joe's level of commitment. Again it comes back to purpose. Joe wanted his team to become the best in the world. It was that purpose, that big *why*, that fuelled his preparation.

The other point to make about preparation is that it takes time to get it right. When Joe Schmidt took over as head coach of Leinster in 2010, the provincial side lost three of their first four games. At the time, many of the pundits wrote him off. One even suggested that he had lost the dressing room. Likewise, when Joe took over the Ireland job in 2013, his first match was an easy win over Samoa, but in the second, the team was soundly beaten by Australia. The successes that would come for both Leinster and Ireland did not come overnight.

Rory puts it like this: 'It takes time to go from learning, to understanding, to the point where it almost becomes automated. But once you understand where you're going, you go there a lot easier because you don't have to think about it. You're not second-guessing yourself.'

The pundits may have decided that Joe's time was up following those early defeats, but his players recognised that he was trying to do something different, and that worthwhile change does not happen quickly. They saw just how much skill, energy and experience was being poured into his preparation, and that gave them the confidence to follow him.

And he always brought so much enthusiasm to that preparation. That's important. Neurologists have found that when you do something with enthusiasm, it takes about one-tenth of the effort needed to do something about which you are unenthusiastic.

'People who are enthusiastic about their work don't feel dragged out at the end of a long day. Instead, when they stop working, they are likely to feel exhilarated.'[1]

Remember too that preparation doesn't remove the risk of failure. The risk of failure is there in any worthwhile endeavour. But preparation reduces that risk like nothing else.

Know When to Stop Preparing

All preparation has to stop at some point. I worked with one client who was brilliant in meetings, who could deliver world-class presentations. The problem was that she invested so much in her preparation that she had no time for anything else. She might put a full day's prep into a half-hour presentation. She delivered, yes, but the cost was simply too high. So we set boundaries, and decided on a ratio of 5:1. Two and a half hours of prep for a half-hour presentation. This time would be focused and distraction-free. Her practice would be concentrated and deliberate. Then she would stop and trust that her own experience and skills, together with that high-grade, focused prep, would deliver for her. And it did. Time and time again.

I've also seen, to my own cost, just how damaging over-preparing can be. During my playing career, I was utterly determined to be the best, and I had no idea that it was possible to over-train, let alone over-think.

In August 2003, Armagh made it to their second All-Ireland football final in a row. This is the biggest event in the Irish sporting calendar: 85,000 people pack the stadium and the match is broadcast to every city in the world. A couple of weeks before the final, a group of us took the week off work and went to Belfast for a gruelling four-day training camp. On top of that, two nights before the final, I went and got some extra individual coaching. I had no conception of the importance of rest and recovery. Years later, I would hear Ronaldo say, 'Too much water kills the plant.' How right he was. I would say now that over-training significantly impacted my performance that September, when we lost the final to Tyrone.

And in my early days on the team, I used to write motivational phrases on my wrist tape: 'Be confident', 'Attack aggressively' and so on. It was silly; it was too much information. I should have trusted the preparation I had done. I should have stopped thinking and started playing. I failed to see the evidence in my past playing career, I failed to see that I was at my best when I just went out and played football and forgot about the rest of the world.

Twenty years later, having coached hundreds of athletes and performers, my advice these days is simple. Do your preparation, but three days out from the challenge, switch off. The computer is programmed. Keep it powered down until an hour before the game.

Not Everyone in a Leadership Position Is a Leader

Some people are great at the big picture. They're blue-sky thinkers who can see the way ahead when others can't. They can motivate and inspire, they're authentic and charismatic and are capable of creating a compelling vision that everyone can rally round. They may be great at values and goals; they may be wonderful speakers. But they'll fail their people if they're bad managers.

You've got to be able to execute. You've got to be able to take that vision, those goals, and use them to schedule and assign tasks day to day.

And you've got to be able to pay the bills. You've got to be punctual.

This all sounds too obvious to mention, but time and again, I've seen those in leadership positions who are bored by the everyday and cannot go from the big picture back to execution.

There has to be implementation of what's been agreed in the plan. There has to be a very significant culture of getting stuff done. There has to be rigour and accountability.

My friend and mentor Michael Dempsey talks about a misstep in his leadership career. While working in the pharmaceutical industry, he and his sales team agreed that they would transform into a high-performing team. They had a series of high-energy, high-commitment meetings, in which they agreed a series of ambitious targets. This was a group of experienced, skilled salespeople, and yet, after three months, Michael realised that no change had taken place. The team was still doing well and achieving sales, but no one was coming near to delivering on the ambitious targets they had agreed in the previous quarter.

He says, 'I called a meeting and explained that I wasn't happy. It was at this point that the truth began to dawn on me. I asked them what exactly it was that we had agreed, and it turned out that each of us had a different view of what a high-performing team was. We had no clarity around it. Now we knew the problem, we were able to create a shared understanding of what a high-performing team was and how it operated. Because they were such talented people, once we all knew where we wanted to go, we wasted no time in getting there.'

You're not finished once that work is done. Every week you sit down with the team and find out where they are in relation to the goals, what resources they need, what blockers exist, what changes need to be made to the plan.

A leader sets that big vision. A leader will inspire, a leader will coach, energise and excite. The leader is there to drive transformation. But they also have to be the manager who makes sure that the team has the tools to execute. A manager is somebody who makes sure the strategy is implemented on the ground. They ensure the right people are in the right seats, doing the right things, right. They ensure that processes are in place and that resource gaps are filled. A manager is somebody who makes sure the results are met. A manager is somebody who, every single day, checks in with their team to make sure they're *getting stuff done*.

Don't underestimate the managerial skill set. American investor John Doerr said, 'Ideas are easy. Execution is everything.' He wasn't wrong.

The very best leaders are also brilliant managers.

About seven years ago, the team and I did an intense 90-day programme formulating our values, our vision and our KPIs (key performance indicators), getting the team aligned and excited and about what we'd achieved and where we were headed. We were just back from a trip working with Digicel in Papua New Guinea that had gone really well. I felt that we had established a brilliant atmosphere, one in which everyone could perform at their very best, knowing that they had the support of the entire team. It was great.

But then one of the team said, 'This is all fine, but what's the plan for *this* week? What are we doing *this* week, to make sure we hit these numbers?'

She went on: 'These goals are great, but what are we doing today to make our customers' lives better? What are we doing today to be better ourselves? What are we doing to make sure that every single time that phone rings, we respond quickly, with courtesy and positivity?'

It's all very well deciding in a meeting to do these things, but without a process to ensure that, the enthusiasm wears off and everyone slides back into the old ways of doing things. It's all very well creating the environment that taps into everyone's creativity, but if people lack the training needed to actually execute, that brilliant atmosphere won't matter.

You don't have the right to be a great leader unless you're a skilled manager. Management and leadership are fundamentally interconnected.

And once you've got a management system in place, that's when you can set your imagination free.

In Summary

- Bad preparation can lead to disaster.

- In victory, the great leaders stay humble and prepare for the next challenge.

- Leaders' preparation builds confidence in their troops. Is your preparation good enough to inspire your team? Your organisation? Your community?

- Know when to stop preparing. Know when you're locked and loaded and ready to go.

- You don't earn the right to be a great leader until you become a great manager.

CHAPTER 9:
CREATIVE THINKING
Unfollow the Rules

When Michael Dempsey was MD of pharma company Bristol Myers Squibb (BMS), he discovered that there was a problem with how cancer care was being delivered in Ireland. Poor communication between the different specialists had led to the development of silos. Many types of cancer can be treated with a combination or sequence of surgery, chemotherapy or radiotherapy, but specialists tended to regard their own discipline as superior, and didn't really value the input of medical experts from what they saw as rival disciplines.

Michael connected with a cancer specialist in St Vincent's Hospital, Professor Niall O'Higgins. Professor O'Higgins believed that better health outcomes would be achieved if care was managed by teams consisting of surgeons, oncologists, oncology nurses and radiologists. By working together, healthcare professionals could develop a holistic plan tailored to the needs of each individual patient. This was how cancer care was handled in the US and there was plenty of data to demonstrate how well it worked.

You'd think that this was such an obvious win that everyone would go for it. What startled Michael was just how difficult it was to break down these silos.

If things have always been done in a particular way, it can be very difficult to instigate change.

> If things have always been done in a particular way, it can be very difficult to instigate change

Michael explains that bringing the various professional groups together required a two-pronged approach: Professor O'Higgins working from within, and Michael and his team working from outside.

'I was very lucky,' says Michael, 'in that I had a strong team in BMS and, in particular, Sean Dowling in the oncology division. Sean was passionate about patient care and worked extremely hard at creating the right environment to bring about change.'

Seminars and conferences were and remain a vital channel for sharing innovations in medicine. The big problem, however, was that despite the fact that the range of cancer care experts – surgeons, oncologists, radiologists – attended these conferences, they tended to be organised along specialist lines, which meant that the different specialties rarely interacted.

Michael believed that the key to breaking down these silos lay in getting everyone talking with each other, getting people to realise that they were not as different as they thought they were.

Professor O'Higgins and the team at BMS worked together to establish the first all-Ireland multidisciplinary breast cancer care conference. Professor O'Higgins brought together a committee comprising senior representatives from each discipline, creating a two-day agenda of content and experience-sharing that focused on the superiority of multi-disciplinary patient care.

When working out the seating arrangements, Michael, Sean and the team made sure that the tables were mixed: oncologists beside radiologists, surgeons beside GPs and so on.

Michael was having coffee with a specialist one morning. He pulled his chair in a little closer and said, 'Michael, you're talking to the wrong people.'

'What? Why?'

'We're the ones you should be talking to. Just us. You're wasting your time having all these meetings.'

Despite this one specialist's prejudice – which was not unrepresentative – the conference was very successful, and would go on to become a major annual event.

'We kept publicising clinical data from the States, which continually showed how much better health outcomes were when medical professionals operated in teams rather than in silos. At the same time Professor O'Higgins in St Vincent's was getting much better results using the same strategy. That made people sit up and listen,' says Michael.

This twin strategy, education and social contact, eventually cracked the problem and today all cancer care in Ireland is team-led.

What's the lesson in all of this?

The first thing that strikes me is that in tackling a problem, you have to engage people who deny that the problem exists at all. This means that you need to think differently. You need to try something new. This is not easy.

Michael Dempsey with his team, and Professor O'Higgins with his, changed things not by hitting people over the head with their clinical data, but by talking to them, and getting them to talk to each other. These interactions built trust and respect, which are vital in the creation of high-performance teams, with good communication skills and the ability to constructively challenge attitudes.

Learning How to Be Late

Remember what schoolteacher Paddy Courtney said in Chapter 2: 'If you teach the same way for ten years, you've only really got one year's experience.' In order to work successfully in a disadvantaged school he had to decommission his thinking. I like that phrase a lot. He had to forget all he had been taught about educational attainment and learning outcomes and completely reinvent his job. Not just his job, but the role of the school.

He talks about teaching kids to be late. This sounds stupid, but hear him out.

'You have to realise that getting into school at all was an heroic effort for many of these kids. They might [have] a row with their mother, they'd have to find their bag and their uniform and maybe wouldn't have had anything to eat, and then they'd arrive in and the teacher would ask, "What do you mean by coming in at this time of the day?" The young lad is already frustrated, now he walks into the room, the whole class stops, everyone turns to look at him so he gives the teacher lip and next thing he's down with the principal and gets sent home. I'd have to teach that kid to say, "Aw, I'm really sorry sir," just so he could placate the teacher and stay in school.'

Later, when he became a principal, Paddy would instruct his own teachers: 'If any kid is late, you welcome them because it's not their fault. I don't care if they come in ten minutes before home time. You thank them.'

One thing I've discovered about many of the most successful leaders I've worked with: at the beginning, what they suggest sounds outlandish, but in the end, they are revealed as the sanest people in the room. My father says that the first time he heard Northern Ireland political leader John Hume stand up and talk about everybody being able to live together in harmony, people looked at him as if he was completely disconnected from reality. And remember from Chapter 1: the best way Kako Bourjolly could find for ensuring that every child got a pair of shoes was by lining them up and carefully outlining each left foot on a separate piece of paper.

This is what leaders do. They find solutions *wherever* those solutions are, and aren't afraid of the ridicule and scorn of people who lack their vision. They're unorthodox because, well, being orthodox hasn't worked. So what looks bizarre at first glance turns out to be the sanest option.

My colleague Eugene Conlon puts it like this: 'If you want to develop yourself, you need to talk to people who are different to you, who think differently to you.' He has a wonderful perspective on fresh think-ing. 'If you sit down and have lunch with exactly the same people every day, you get no new ideas, you get no new ways of looking at things. You sit down with somebody who has a dif-ferent way of thinking, who looks at life differently, who's a ballerina, who's an artist, who's a musician – they'll inspire new ways of thinking, they'll bring gems into your head.'

Leaders find solutions *wherever* those solutions are, and aren't afraid of the ridicule and scorn of people who lack their vision

Gems into your head. That's good.

Where did Henry Ford get the idea for creating the world's first assembly line? In a Chicago slaughterhouse.[1] He watched the carcasses, mounted on a monorail, move from one worker to the next, and that sparked an idea that was to revolutionise the motor industry. I don't know what he was doing there, but I do know that this was someone whose mind was open, and who was prepared to find the germ of a brilliant idea anywhere.

Kevin Roberts, in his book *64 Shots: Leadership in a Crazy World,* says this: 'We need to move away from thinking about the world being Volatile, Uncertain, Complex and Ambiguous and move, with a growth mindset, to perceive a super-VUCA world, i.e. Vibrant, Unreal, Crazy and Astounding!'[2]

I like that idea, and it's an idea that successful leaders are starting to embrace.

Bill Taylor wrote a piece in the November 2017 edition of the *Harvard Business Review* about how companies like Coca-Cola learn from failure. Earlier that year, after James Quincey became CEO of Coca-Cola, one of the first things he set out to tackle was what he called a 'culture of cautiousness', which dogged the company since the 'New Coke' fiasco of 1985. Back then, the rise in popularity of other soft drinks prompted the company to change their formula, but New Coke was a disaster and the old recipe was reinstated within three months. This embarrassing u-turn lingered long in the memory and, in Quincey's mind, was responsible for Coke's reluctance to take risks, to innovate. He said, 'If we're not making mistakes, we're not trying hard enough.'[3]

This isn't to say that making mistakes is good, or that being sloppy is in any way acceptable. It's simply that being overcautious kills innovation. Mistakes and wrong turnings can be excellent sources of learning and improvement and need to be seen as such.

Be Brave

Lorraine Culligan of Primark was well positioned to see the havoc that the COVID pandemic unleashed. As the dust settled, she saw a crisis of leadership in so many areas across the corporate world.

'Fatigue has set in and leaders are struggling to manage themselves. I think a global rebuilding of leadership is required, particularly for companies that went through real challenges during the pandemic, those whose businesses were on their knees.'

Leaders are struggling, she points out, because they're always-on, because they haven't had a proper holiday. Burnout is becoming a serious problem again.

'If you're in back-to-back meetings all the time, if your diary is jam-packed, something's wrong. It's like a badge of honour: *I'm so busy!* As a leader in my organisation, I want to strip that back. I want to ask what are all these meetings for? Who's accountable? How do we make decisions faster?'

This culture of overwork isn't just a problem for now, she points out, it's a problem for the future too.

'How do we make leadership something that people want to aspire to? You've got the next generation of leaders looking at leaders who may not be displaying the right behaviours right now.'

This, she believes, is part of the reason for the great resignation. The leaders of the future are looking at overburdened managers and saying, 'Hang on a second, if that's what leadership is about, I don't want any of it.'

This culture of overwork isn't just a problem for now, it's a problem for the future too

The solution?

'You have to be brave. You really have to be brave as a leader. You have to challenge a situation that's simply unsustainable. And the next generation of leaders has to be brave, too. They have to challenge their leaders. They have to ask hard questions. And organisations have to give space to people to allow that challenge to happen.'

She points to a kind of fragility that's crept into leadership since the pandemic.

'There's a lot of sensitivity out there at the moment, which makes people shy about giving their opinion. But that should not be the culture of any organisation. If you've got an opinion, you shouldn't need to get approval to speak up.'

Part of the problem stems from the fact that relationships have been strained by remote working and physical distancing. Breaking down those barriers will allow relationships to strengthen, rebuilding trust and reducing those sensitivities. That way, we can start to challenge each other respectfully again.

'People have missed out by not being together. How does somebody really show up on a screen? If I'm sitting with you, if we're sharing the same physical space, I can look you in the eye. In the next few weeks, we will have the first physical meeting of our group of leaders since the pandemic. I'm really looking forward to getting them together physically to network, to talk to each other. I'm looking forward to having honest, robust conversations with that group of leaders about expectations, about supportive leadership and accountability.'

She believes too that in this post-pandemic world, leadership needs to be reinvented.

'Throw it up in the air. *Think* about it differently. Because the answers aren't quite as obvious as they were before.'

That process has to be inclusive. We have to hear the voices of tomorrow's leaders. We have to know what they would like to see from today's leaders. We need to be communicating continually, and to everybody. Leadership can't become elitist.

'It can't be, "Oh, you have to be in the top 200 to be a leader." No, you don't. Everybody leads within their own area.'

Everything You Need You Already Have

You would think that the most fertile ground for creativity comes when there are no restrictions, when you're free to dream up whatever it is you want to dream up. In practice, however, the reverse is actually true.

Brendan McGurgan, former CEO of CDE Global, talks about how the global financial crisis taught him and his team to be more creative just to survive. He introduced a range of process innovations that would, in time, transform the company from a small, twenty-person, locally focused operation to the biggest wet-processing machinery supplier in the world. But in late 2008, the company's order pipeline dried up almost overnight. Brendan worked out that he needed to reduce overheads by £35,000 per month just to keep the doors open. The obvious thing to do here would be to reduce headcount. Brendan did not want to do this. Instead, he placed this challenge in front of the senior team.

'I told them that I needed £35,000 in monthly savings. They asked for seven days to try to figure it out, and one week later, I sat with the board as the team presented what they called Project 35. They proposed a range of innovations, which included a reduction in their salaries but did not include any reduction in head count. No one lost their job.'

That there is a masterclass in leadership.

Brendan did not set out to solve this problem on his own (you can't do it alone). He didn't try to be a hero. He communicated the problem clearly and honestly. He invited the senior team to collaborate to find a way for all of them to continue to work together. By communicating the full unvarnished truth, he let them know that he trusted them to come up with a solution. By communicating a reluctance to let anyone go, he set the tone for a compassionate solution.

Here's what I learned from that: great leaders are not heroes. They are hero-makers.

Great leaders are not heroes. They are hero-makers

The other thing I take away from this experience is if Brendan had said, 'Go away and figure out how to reduce costs,' I don't think he'd have achieved the same level of engagement or collegiality. 'Figure out how to reduce costs' is woolly, it's vague, it's meh. I think it would have inspired nothing but a shopping list of possibilities. By telling them that they needed to cut £35,000 per month, that constraint actually set them free to zero in on precise measures that could be introduced immediately.

I've seen this time and again, in all walks of life and in all kinds of contexts. Remember Shackleton and his crew, stranded on Elephant Island with no hope of rescue? As he stood on the shore of that barren, windswept island, Shackleton knew that he had to create some means of travelling across 800 miles of treacherous ocean, and do it with nothing but the meagre resources before him.

So what did he do? How did they prepare? Carpenter Harry McNeish cut the mast from one of the smaller boats and fitted it to the keel of the boat they would take – the *James Caird* – to prevent it buckling in heavy seas. Corkman Tim McCarthy figured out a way of constructing a covering for the boat, using the lids of cases and the four sledge runners that were lashed inside the boat. McNeish completed the covering with canvas – which first had to be thawed out on a stove fuelled by seal blubber. This was cut and sewn by two more of the men before it was nailed into place.[4]

Everything Shackleton and his men needed to survive the monstrous challenges that lay ahead, they already had. That's the essence of creative constraint. Using what you've got to get you where you need to go.

Shackleton, as you'll have seen by now, is one of my heroes. He is the historic leader I look to most often for inspiration and example. His resilience, his creativity, his unique ability to lead shines on 100 years after his death. Ultimately, however, when it came to the moonshot goals he set himself, he failed. I want to look at *why* he failed next.

In Summary

- Radical thinking can revolutionise your organisation, just like it did for cancer care in Ireland.
- Teach your children how to be late for school.
- Being always-on is giving us nothing but leader burn-out; we need to rethink the overwork culture if we want to inspire a new generation of leaders.
- Sometimes imposing constraints unlocks powerful creativity.

CHAPTER 10:

DIVERSITY

The Need for Other Voices

Shackleton never got to the South Pole, let alone became the first to get there. His mission on *Endurance* was to cross Antarctica from sea to sea, via the pole. The story of that voyage tells you so much about great leadership in adversity, but you can't ignore the fact that it is also a story of failure. *Endurance* was destroyed by ice and its crew marooned before they came anywhere near to achieving their goal. To be clear, the fact that he failed to get there doesn't undermine Shackleton's extraordinary – and successful – rescue of his crew, but you can't pretend that he didn't fail to do what he set out to do.

I think that the reason Shackleton didn't reach his goal is the same reason that the greatest polar explorer of all time, Roald Amundsen, succeeded. Amundsen beat both Scott and Shackleton to the South Pole. Before that, he had been the first person to navigate the Northwest Passage, which is the North American sea route between the Atlantic and the Pacific. Why did he succeed where others failed? I think it's because he had an entirely different mindset to either Scott or Shackleton.

In Amundsen's biography *The Last Viking*, Stephen Brown says that the Norwegian rejected the 'British-empire-against-the-world'[1] style of exploration and instead approached his goals as physical and mental challenges.

Born into a seafaring family, Amundsen had been fascinated by polar exploration since he was a child. In particular, he was fascinated by the tragic fate of Captain John Franklin, whose ships and crew were lost in a doomed attempt to find the Northwest passage. Amundsen first studied medicine, but it was his mother's ambition that he become a doctor, and when she died, he immediately changed tack and pursued a maritime career. He spent years building up Arctic and Antarctic experience before buying the 21-metre sloop *Gjøa* in 1901. The next five months were spent with the boat's existing crew, learning everything he could about how it handled in Arctic waters. It was already quite an old ship – it had been built in 1872 – so he had it strengthened and restored.

Now he needed a crew, but in stark contrast to those famous English expeditions of the previous century, Amundsen hired only six men. This was lean production years before the Japanese developed the idea. During the previous century, the British Admiralty had poured huge sums of money and manpower into the fruitless search for the Northwest passage. The doomed Franklin expedition included two ships, a fully stocked library of over 1,000 books, over 8,000 food tins and several live cattle. And yet, neither they, nor any of the 129 men who crewed the ships, survived. Amundsen learned from those excesses, and reasoned that travelling light made far more sense than bringing the world with you.

Writing in *Canadian Geographic* in June 2018, Amundsen expert Geir O. Kløver explained that Amundsen wanted a small and tight-knit crew on board *Gjøa*, 'who would all have plenty to do during the expedition and who could, to some extent, live off the land and handle the challenges of Arctic life'.[2]

In September of 1903, he sailed into the Simpson Strait on Canada's central Arctic coast, but rather than strike out for the passage right away, he decided to remain there for two years, in order to take magnetic readings. Locating the magnetic North Pole was another key target for explorers and scientists of that time. While he was wintering in the harbour, a small group of Inuit arrived and established a village nearby. These people had never seen a white man before, but Amundsen approached them and established friendly relations, to the point where the Norwegian crew learned the Inuit language and were able to communicate freely with them. The Inuit taught Amundsen and his team how to make igloos, drive dogs and dress warmly in loose furs.

In return, the Norwegians gave the Inuit knives, needles, matches and even food. They hunted together and spent time in each other's camps. During those two years, Amundsen and his six-man crew became experts in surviving in one of the most hostile places on earth. They discovered that between -30 and -60 degrees, the tents they had brought were cold and damp, while the igloos – built from nothing but snow – were windproof and dry. In his diary, Amundsen wrote that he stopped using his old clothes and wore only Inuit clothing, and that the snow goggles they had brought from Norway were useless compared to the ones given to them by the locals.

Amundsen and his crew set out to look for the passage in June 1903, hugging the shore and threading their way through to the other side, often through water that was less than a metre deep. They anchored at Herschel Island in the Beaufort Sea – which leads out into the Pacific – and Amundsen skied for 500 miles across wild and frozen land to the city of Eagle in Alaska, to telegraph that he and his team had succeeded.

By the time he was ready to turn his attention to the race for the South Pole six years later, Amundsen could hardly have been better prepared. Once again, he chose a small team of nineteen men. By contrast, Robert Falcon Scott, whose party set off for the South Pole five weeks after Amundsen, brought a crew of sixty-five. Once they established their Antarctic base, Amundsen's team used dogs and skis to cross the terrain. Scott relied on ponies and motor sledges – neither of which proved particularly effective. Both parties suffered setbacks, but it was Amundsen's apprenticeship with the Inuit six years earlier that made all the difference. His team, travelling light, reached the pole thirty-four days before Scott. Imagine the disappointment Scott must have felt when he arrived at the pole only to find Amundsen's black flag flying there. And, of course, Scott, together with the four-man team he took with him on the final push for the pole, perished on the return journey.

Amundsen and all of his men made it back safely.

Diversity and Innovation

Today, the most cutting-edge organisations and companies recognise that innovation simply doesn't happen without diversity.

Douglas Terrier is NASA's chief technologist. He says: 'As NASA looks to the future, we're investigating and incorporating the best innovative practices from within and outside the government to enable our future missions and advance America's economic competitiveness. Part of a successful culture of innovation is recognising and embracing a diverse and inclusive workforce.'[3]

Then there's Google's X – the Moonshot Factory. They've set their sights on having a ten-times impact on the world's most intractable problems. For example: 'Malta' is a grid-scale renewable energy storage technology that stores electricity as heat in large tanks of molten salt. 'Wing' is an autonomous delivery drone which aims to reduce traffic congestion and ease carbon dioxide transport emissions. The team at X aims for these incredible goals by adopting the speed, risk-profile and ambition of a start-up.

Here's the fourth of their ten tips for moonshot takers: 'The myth of the lone genius inventor with a single eureka moment is just that: a myth. Innovation happens when teams of people from diverse communities, cultures and disciplines come together, challenging each other to spark even better ideas. When assembling a team, ask yourself whether each person's background lends itself to a unique point of view, or might just mirror someone else's. People who've travelled wildly divergent paths can break each other out of ruts and generate creative connections that aren't likely otherwise.'[4]

It makes sense when you think about it. You get a talented pool of people from diverse backgrounds to circle a problem, they're all going to think differently. They're all going to come at it from a different angle. If you want the same old answers, ask the same old people the same old questions. Captain Franklin failed and Robert Scott failed not because they lacked the fortitude to overcome the obstacles that polar exploration posed. Rather, they failed to see value in any culture but their own.

If you want the same old answers, ask the same old people the same old questions

Diverse groups are less prone to groupthink, which is the phenomenon where people suspend their own beliefs and common sense in order to arrive at a consensus solution. Writing in 2019, British journalist and author Matthew Syed argued that the CIA's failure to prevent the 9/11 attacks was caused, in part, by the lack of diversity in its staff. The agency's recruitment processes were excellent, drawing in the very best of the best, but almost all were members of the white male elite. Syed says, 'If you bring a group of people who share similar perspectives and backgrounds, they are liable to share the same blind spots. And this means that far from challenging and addressing these blind spots, they are likely to be reinforced.'[5]

A lot of organisations out there are getting diversity right. Lenovo, which employs 57,000 people across sixty companies, is now the biggest PC vendor in the world. In January 2022, the company was awarded a perfect score of 100 in the 2022 Corporate Equality Index, earning it the distinction of being a 'best place to work for LGBTQ equality'.[6]

'Qualification for the index is based upon a company's adoption of LGBTQ-related policies and practices, including non-discrimination, workplace protections, domestic partner benefits, transgender-inclusive health-care benefits, competency programmes and public engagement with the LGBTQ community.'[7]

This was the fifth year in a row in which the company achieved a perfect score, and it's also heartening to know that Lenovo was one of no fewer than 842 businesses that earned a perfect score in 2022.

One more thing about Lenovo. In both 2012 and 2013, chairman and CEO of the company Yang Yuanqing redistributed his €3-million-plus bonus between some 10,000 of Lenovo's staff.[8]

That's leadership.

Leadership That Transforms

Over the last two decades, research into the human brain has found less and less evidence that there are significant differences between male and female brains. Lise Eliot is a professor of neuroscience at Rosalind Franklin University of Medicine and Science in Chicago. She says that except for the difference in size, 'there are no meaningful differences between men's and women's brain structure or activity that hold up across diverse populations.'[9]

Mary Collins asks this question: 'If it's not a biological trait, then what is it? It's the socio-cultural dimension: how we've been formed and brought up. Or, if you want to put it another way, it's nurture rather than nature.'

She explains that Rochemartin's Emotional Capital Framework divides emotional intelligence into ten core competencies. 'Here, the research tells us that there are some very slight, and I mean very slight, differences between males and females. Women score very slightly higher on empathy and relationship skills and men score slightly higher on self-confidence and self-control.'

There are many different models and frameworks of leadership out there, but for my money, the most powerful is transformational leadership. It was first theorised by James McGregor Burns in the seventies, and refined again by Bernard Bass in the eighties. Transformational leadership is all about mentoring and inspiring those you lead into becoming leaders themselves. Again: great leaders are not heroes. They are hero-makers. It's about being values-based, being authentic, being compassionate. Think Martin Luther King, think Nelson Mandela.

Because women score more highly on empathy and relationship skills, they tend to be more skilled at transformational leadership. During the COVID crisis, for example, it was the world's female leaders who were most effective in bringing people with them. Premiers such as Germany's Angela Merkel, New Zealand's Jacinda Ardern, Denmark's Mette Frederiksen, Taiwan's Tsai Ing-wen and Finland's Sanna Marin drew positive media attention for their approach to the pandemic, and the public support they enjoyed as a result. Their successes aren't simply anecdotal, however. A 2021 analysis of 194 countries published by the Centre for Economic Policy Research and the World Economic Forum found that countries led by women had 'systematically and significantly better' COVID-19 outcomes than those led by men. The research shows that they actually suffered half as many deaths.[10]

Despite all this, women remain seriously under-represented in leadership roles. Ninety per cent of heads of state and Fortune 500 CEOs are men. We talked in Chapter 2: *Self-Awareness* about imposter syndrome and the fact that it is experienced by disproportionately larger numbers of high-performing women.

There are of course many reasons for the fact that there are not enough women leaders, but one of the most significant, in my view, is that despite the evidence that women are, if anything, more suited to leadership roles, our culture doesn't encourage women to step up.

Mary Collins tells this story: 'I spoke to a senior female partner about the under-representation of women in leadership roles and she had what I've found to be a very common reaction. She said, "Well, Mary, women make choices. Women want to be at home with their children." I really don't believe it's that simple. The studies show that typically about 5–10 per cent of women want to give up their careers and be at home. This gives their lives purpose. That's great. I admire those women hugely. Then there's another 5–10 per cent that say this motherhood thing is not for me, and that's perfectly fine too. Most of us, however – some 80 per cent of women

– want to be great parents *and* want to have a successful career. We want to blend both. So I don't think it's good enough to say women make choices. As a society, we have to support women to enable them to take on these leadership positions.'

Part of the solution lies in increasing the number of male advocates for female involvement in leadership roles. The UN's HeForShe solidarity movement for gender equality is an excellent initiative. It provides a platform on which men and boys can engage and become change agents towards the achievement of gender equality. It invites them to build on the work of the women's movement as equal partners, crafting and implementing a shared vision of gender equality that will benefit all of humanity.

Inclusion

Remember too that just because you've got a diverse team does not mean that it is inclusive. We'll be talking about psychological safety in Chapter 13, but for now it's enough to know that if the atmosphere isn't right, those diverse voices will not be heard.

'When you get diversity and inclusion together, then the team is going to perform at their best,' says Katrina Steady. 'They are going to put their best work out there and that is ultimately what we want, right?'

Lorraine Culligan of Primark says that in her organisation everything was seen through the eyes of leaders based in Ireland and the UK.

'That was relevant then, but as we expand, we have to

think about leadership differently, we have to think about our culture differently. Globally, we have our framework and principles, but we also have to appreciate the importance of doing business the local way and understanding those cultural differences.'

She points out that this transition begins by asking questions.

'How do you do business the local way? How do you incorporate local culture? How does that fit into your diversity and inclusion [D&I] agenda? Your communications agenda? We're asking different questions of ourselves and bringing people together to think about culture in a very different way.'

In the past, she says, we might have assumed we knew the answers. Today, we know that we have to listen more. To take one example: the company is currently working on developing family-friendly policies across the group.

'Right now, we're bringing people-leaders from the different markets to look at these policies through the eyes of their particular market. That takes a lot of work because these different critiques and nuances need to be taken on board. It can't work until everyone signs off. I think in the past we would have done something in this area, ticked it off and thought, great, job done, that policy is ready to go. We've realised that we need consultation with local leaders. Otherwise, they're just not going to get behind it. It takes an awful lot more work, but it pays off in the long run.'

We'll be talking about communication next, but it's worth pointing out here that clear communication is so important when you are interacting across cultures.

'Simplicity is a vital principle,' says Lorraine. 'Let's keep things simple. Now that sounds easy, but it is not. No jargon. Get to the point and get there quickly. And we've found too that things often get lost in translation, so the text has to be clear enough so that you don't get translation issues.'

Living in a diverse world *can* create communication problems. Nobody wants to give offence, but offence is often given. Katrina Steady acknowledges that this is a very touchy topic right now. 'You've heard of the golden rule, where we want to treat others as we want to be treated. That doesn't work anymore. It's really about the *platinum* rule: treat others the way *they* want to be treated.'

So you've got to get to know people and find out how they want to be treated, how they want to be addressed, how they want to be communicated with.

This isn't about political correctness or legal compliance. It's about recognising that everyone deserves to work in a safe and inclusive environment, one that allows them to contribute meaningfully, that recognises our differences and our potential. It's about putting together a team of individuals who love being part of a team that both challenges and supports them.

We all want to be part of something great.

In Summary

- Learn from the experts first and fast. Roald Amundsen was open to learning from those who lived in the most inhospitable places on earth, and so succeeded where all others failed.

- Don't lose sight of the close link between innovation and diversity.

- A lack of diversity can lead first to groupthink, then to disaster.

- Strive to have capable female leaders and diverse voices at all levels of your organisation.

- Diversity is not the same as inclusion. Make sure all voices are heard.

CHAPTER II:
COMMUNICATION
Shut Up and Listen

You think of communication, you think oratory, you think marketing, branding and PR. But the most important element of communication, to my mind, is silence. I'm continually amazed at the fact that of the many leaders I've worked with over the years, very few of them are good listeners. And yet being able to listen is the most critical skill set for any leader.

Seamus Mallon was famous for his stubbornness and the force of his personality, but remember too that he was the SDLP's chief negotiator during the talks that ultimately led to the Good Friday Agreement. I asked him once about his tactics as a negotiator. By that time, I'd read countless books on negotiation, and had taken a range of courses in negotiation techniques. Seamus, by contrast, had led *actual* negotiations, with everyone from the IRA to the British government. His advice was disarmingly simple.

'If you want to negotiate with people that have very strong opinions and very strong opposing opinions, you do three vitally important things. Listen, listen and listen.'

Why are good listeners so hard to find? Because listening – real, active listening – is hard. Really hard.

People speak too fast or too slow. They mumble, they're too aggressive, or not aggressive enough. They might not be fluent in your language. A team member with excellent skills in other areas may not be a skilled communicator, and may fail to get their ideas across. Susan Cain, author of *Quiet: The Power of Introverts in a World that Can't Stop Talking*, says that studies in group dynamics suggest that we tend to think that talkative people are more intelligent, better-looking and more likeable than their quieter counterparts.[1]

'The more a person talks, the more other group members direct their attention to her, which means that she becomes increasingly powerful as a meeting goes on. It also helps to speak fast; we rate quick talkers as more capable and appealing than slow talkers.'[2]

The other issue is that we're all so easily distracted. Everyone is busy. Your next meeting, this morning's argument with your spouse, the need to book the car in for a service, that nagging pain in your shoulder … all of these things are continually competing for your attention. Also, we can think much faster than we can speak. So when someone is talking to us – particularly someone who speaks slowly – we have a lot of left-over brain power. Within a few minutes of the beginning of a conversation, it's very easy to become distracted and to start ruminating on other things.

Next time you're in conversation with three or more people, notice how little attention is being paid to the speaker. Yes, you hear what they're saying, but most of our processing capacity is given over to preparing for what we're about to say, and trying to identify the best moment in which to take our turn to speak.

Neither politeness nor turn-taking are the same thing as listening.

Ego is part of the problem too. So is the misguided belief that communication is a one-way street. The leader thinks that in order to motivate, they have to continually deliver instructions and inspiration. The truth, however, is that we need a constant flow of communication *from* the team to the leader. Sometimes, when someone takes up a leadership position, even if they don't physically remove themselves from their team, an invisible barrier springs up between them. Unless the leader takes steps to ensure that they remain plugged in to the challenges and aspirations of those they lead, they run the risk of becoming detached and aloof.

Leaders who fail to put feedback loops in place won't realise what they're missing. This is a particular issue in hierarchical organisations. If there's no culture of telling the leader that they're not listening, the leader becomes ever more detached. They have moved so far up the totem pole that people no longer feel capable of saying, 'You're not listening to me.'

Listening

I'm going to define listening as the ability to create a safe environment in which the person you're communicating with is able to tell you what you need to be told. What it requires more than anything else is time and respect. If you want to really connect with someone, if you want them to open up to you and tell you the truth, you need to give them time in which to do that. Not everyone will be ready to talk truthfully in a five-minute window. By making the time to listen, you're telling them that you value them, that you value their input.

Listening is not passive, it's the process of active, compassionate engagement. Listening requires focus, it requires an awareness of the other person, not just of the words coming out of their mouth, but also *how* they're saying what they're saying. You need to watch their body language, their overall demeanour. Are they up? Are they down? Are they nervous? Reserved or exuberant? What are they *really* telling you? Are they holding something back? I like that Elizabeth Gilbert quote: 'Listen to the whispers or soon you'll be listening to the screams.'

Listening is not a box-ticking exercise: *Right, I've listened to the team, now let's get back to the important stuff.* It is the important stuff. It's not about you saying, 'OK, tell me what you think.' It's all about you creating the right conditions for them to tell you what they *really* think. There's a difference.

Good-quality listening is even more difficult now that so many of our interactions happen remotely. Katrina Steady points out that when we're in video meetings, we're far more likely to multi-task.

'People can tell', she says, 'when you're just not listening to them.'

And of course, it's when we're distant from each other that we are most prone to feelings of isolation. That's when you have to step up and work even harder to make sure you're not disconnected from your team, or from what Katrina calls 'your squad' – that is, the people *you* rely on for connection.

'Ask the right questions so that you get to know the team on a deeper level. We all ask, "How are you doing?" but really that's too broad, too general. Go deeper. Ask more specific questions: "Tell me what you did on the weekend." "How is your family doing?" "Give me one word to describe your current state of mind." That one word can lead to much more meaningful communication than a throwaway "How are you?"'

And good listening doesn't end when the interaction is over. If you've been given feedback, you have to act on it. You have to be seen to be responding. Nodding and smiling and taking notes as someone talks to you is necessary, but it's not enough.

In Chapter 6: *No Ego* Rory Best talked about how he learned that as captain he did not have to have the last word, that he could share the burden of leadership among the team and thereby empower others and harness the strength of the group.

Beware too of the risks attached to speaking first.

As the leader, you have to be aware of your status within the group. Even if you try to keep structures flat, if you are the first to speak, you will set the agenda, you will set the limits on creativity. You will implicitly invite people to agree with you. If you speak first, chances are that all you'll hear back are variations of what you've said. You'll make it harder for those with fresh ideas to speak up.

And when someone finishes talking, wait. Don't rush in with your response. The very best interviewers are the ones who aren't afraid of silence.

I also like this insight from a 2015 *Guardian* interview with Nobel Laureate Daniel Kahneman: 'Meetings (should) start with participants writing down their ideas about the issue at hand before anyone speaks. That way, the halo effect – whereby the concerns raised first and most assertively dominate the discussion – can be mitigated, and a range of views considered.'[3]

During the Second World War, the US Naval Service produced a booklet: *Standard Submarine Phraseology*, which set out how verbal commands would be given on the Atlantic submarine fleet. Because the word 'third' sounds so much like 'first', the former was replaced with 'thuh-ree'. Similarly, the word 'close' (as in close the door) was replaced by the word 'shut' to stop it being confused with the word 'blow'.[4] Brevity was important, so all excess words were removed – no room for 'sir' or 'please' or 'thank you'. The most crucial part of ensuring that orders were understood, however, was repetition. Whoever took the order was required to repeat it back word for word to ensure that it had been understood.

You may not be taking orders on a submarine in a theatre of war, but that idea – repeating back what you've heard to ensure that you've understood what's being said to you – is golden. If a member of the team shares critical information with you, if they feed back to you, or seek your help in some way, make sure you both leave the meeting with a shared understanding of what's been said. If appropriate, follow up with an email confirming the content of the meeting and the action steps that fall from it.

Listening Groups

Lorraine Culligan of Primark discovered during the pandemic that keeping the lines of communication open across the organisation is vital, even when there's nothing to say.

'There were times when we arranged town-hall meetings despite [there being] nothing new to tell anyone. But by going out and being honest with people, by saying how we felt as the leadership team and showing genuine interest in their welfare – that made a big difference. For me, from a leadership perspective, communication is vital.'

In the post-pandemic world in which I write, companies everywhere are struggling to find the right blend of remote and onsite working. Some favour a mandatory return-to-work, others favour remote working, with every sort of combination in between. Figuring out the right blend is causing a lot of conflict. Not in Primark, however.

'During the pandemic, we had our head-office functions in Dublin and regional-office colleagues across all of our markets suddenly working from home. As the restrictions eased, we had to think about what the new normal would look like.

I remember at a town-hall meeting with our head-office colleagues, this landed into the chat box: *We don't want to go back to the office five days a week. Are you going force us?* The question caught me off-guard. I knew I had to be careful about how I answered, but in the end I was honest. I said I didn't know. I said: "The first thing we have to do is talk to each other. Listen to everyone's opinion. I don't know the answer right now, but we'll work on it together."

'On the back of that interaction, we set up listening groups and found out what people wanted and how they imagined work in the future. Then we pulled all of that information together, got a team within the people and culture team on it, engaged with our leaders and came back with a framework for hybrid working. When we launched it, people were amazed at how far we'd gone. The response from our people was overwhelmingly positive, all because we had communicated so well around a topic that was clearly causing a lot of anxiety. People felt that they got to say what they had to say, they felt listened to. And because we listened to them, we were able to introduce a meaningful solution.'

'That doesn't happen by chance. If we had said, "Everybody has to be here," there would have been resistance. We understood that the old way of working was gone, and that we needed to create something new. That collaborative approach and inclusiveness created the right atmosphere and we're now seeing the highest level of attendance since the pandemic began.'

Precision, Economy, Clarity

Joe Schmidt was one of the best communicators I've ever worked with. I talked before about the level of preparation he brought to every new challenge. It was the same with communication. In every meeting, he would break down the plays he had created into their constituent parts and explain them in a way that left no one in any doubt about either what they were being asked to do or why they were being asked to do it. It was a masterclass in communication.

Long before he was appointed Ireland coach – back in the summer of 2010 – Joe took over as Leinster Rugby head coach after three years working as assistant coach with Clermont in France. I was performance coach with Leinster at the time. At his very first meeting, he articulated his goal for Leinster: they would become the best team in Europe at passing the ball.

This surprised me. I remember looking around to see what other people made of this oddly specific goal, but almost at once I began to see the brilliance of it. Typically, when a new coach arrives into a team, he'll try to wow them with superlatives: *we'll become the best team in Europe, playing creative, expansive, heads-up rugby.* Joe didn't do that.

Great communication will always tick three boxes: it will be clear, it will be precise and it will be economical: clarity, precision, economy. A sweeping, grandiose vision might be clear and economically articulated, but Joe's vision for the team brought that third characteristic to the party. It was *so* precise. There are many ways to play creative, expansive, heads-up rugby, but by zoning in on one thing, he was able to sweep away all the ambiguity and rally the team around a simple collective goal.

As I've already mentioned, Joe didn't have the easiest of starts with Leinster. The team lost three of their first four games. What was interesting, though, was that despite the fact that many of those outside the squad had begun to write him off, inside the collective, there wasn't any dissent. He brought a new level of rigour to training, a new emphasis on getting the basics right, getting the preparation right, getting the processes right.

The other key point to make here is that the brilliant articulation of a vision is only one part of the puzzle. As the weeks passed, the players saw first-hand just how much preparation Joe put into each match, they saw the logic in what he proposed. They saw that he was both sincere and honest. He was the real deal. That, more than anything else, is why they bought in.

In other words, you can't fake this stuff. You have to be seen to be living and breathing the words you've said. Otherwise the whole thing will fall apart.

> You have to be seen to be living and breathing the words you've said. Otherwise the whole thing will fall apart

Before Joe progressed to become head coach with the Irish rugby team, Leinster won back-to-back European Cups in 2011 and 2012. While they got knocked out of the European Cup in the group stages in 2013, Schmidt's Leinster won both the Challenge Cup and the Pro12 trophy that year.

Being articulate helps, no question. If the leader can't make what they're trying to say clear, they're in trouble right away. But it's more important to be real. If you can deliver a brilliant speech but don't live by it, you're done, you've failed.

Harness the Power of Stories

We've been telling each other stories for tens of thousands of years. They connect with something deep within the human psyche, which is why there is no more powerful way of illustrating an insight than by telling a story built around it. Stories are uniquely memorable; they remain in the mind long after theory and advice have been forgotten. If you can share a personal experience that captures the essence of what you want people to know, you are elevating your capacity for communication immeasurably.

Shortly after the collapse of Lehman Brothers – the event that heralded the 2008 global financial crisis – I got a call from renowned Irish communication expert Tom Savage. Tom, who's sadly no longer with us, had a long and illustrious career, in which he advised a who's who of politicians and businesspeople. He asked me to help out on a series of leadership workshops with an international bank that had of course been hit hard by the emerging crisis.

'These workshops are going to be about mindset, resilience and emotional intelligence,' he told me, 'but more importantly they will be about supporting these people through probably the toughest time in their professional lives.'

The bank was undergoing a massive reorganisation. We were told that as many as 50 per cent of those we would be working with would have their contracts terminated, while those left behind would have their jobs radically altered. Salaries would be reduced and bonuses withdrawn.

Our first session was in New York, on the twentieth floor of a Fifth Avenue office complex. I'll never forget the atmosphere when Tom and I walked into the room that morning. The air was thick with dejection and anger. Twenty-five senior managers, some slumped in their chairs, doodling idly; others sitting with legs and arms crossed, scowling up at us. There was a fragility about them; you wouldn't know whether they were about to punch you or burst into tears. I'd run countless leadership workshops at this stage and had developed a keen sense of just how open and teachable an audience was. This room, was, without doubt, the least engaged I'd ever encountered. Not that I blamed them. They were, as Tom had already pointed out, facing an extraordinarily difficult time.

Tom – who was into his seventies at this stage – began his introduction. His demeanour was very different from everyone else in the room. He was upbeat, his body language open, his voice clear and strong. He began with a story, a story about himself. He had been diagnosed with stomach cancer some years earlier. He talked about the doctors, the treatment, the uncertain prognoses, his despair and how he had found the resilience to come through the experience. As he spoke, I watched the mood in the room slowly transform. The doodling stopped. Arms and legs uncrossed. People began to sit up, to hang on his every word. He brought the story to a conclusion with Victor Frankl's liberating insight: 'Everything can be taken from a man but one thing: the last of the human freedoms – to choose one's attitude in any given set of circumstances, to choose one's own way.'[5]

'Now ladies and gentlemen,' he said, '*you* have a choice. How do you choose to respond to this crisis? Is it the end of your career? Do you choose to wallow in despair for the next year? Or do you choose to reinvent yourself? Are you going to do something about it?'

This story became the launchpad for what turned out to be one of the best workshops I'd ever facilitated.

Never underestimate the power of story to connect with people, and to connect them with fundamental truths.

In Summary

- The first step in great communication is shutting up.

- Listening is the ability to create a safe environment in which the person you're communicating with is able to tell you what you need to be told.

- When you decide a course of action, make sure that everyone understands exactly what has been agreed and the actions that flow from it.

- Honesty and keeping the lines of communication open can prove extremely powerful when tough decisions need to be made.

- All great communication is based on three principles: clarity, economy and precision.

- Harness the power of storytelling to deliver memorable insights.

CHAPTER 12:

COLLABORATION

It's All About Trust

Playing against the All Blacks in 2013, Rory Best broke his arm. He heard a pop and looked down to see his hand dangling uselessly. His arm would no longer do what it was told. But the injury hadn't been spotted, and so there was no break in play. The Irish defensive line was under fierce pressure, the All Blacks were attacking in waves. Next thing, Ireland turned the ball over, right in front of him, then one of the All Blacks came diving in to poach it back. As pain began to sear up his arm, Rory's instincts took over and he drove the player back and cleaned the ball – meaning he protected it for the Irish forwards. I was in the stands that day. I saw it and I couldn't believe it. He dived into a situation that most people wouldn't go near in the full of their health, let alone with a broken arm.

Rory is one of the toughest, most committed and intelligent

athletes I've ever worked with, and yet he admitted to feeling deep insecurity when Joe Schmidt first took over as head coach with Ireland. Joe was graduating from a Leinster team that had won everything. It stood to reason, then, that he would favour the Leinster players that he knew and trusted. Rory was an outsider in that he was one of the few members of the Ulster contingent on the squad. When you don't know where you stand, you tend to focus on the negative. Rory, by his own admission, had never been a great ball-carrier, and knew for a fact that this had worked against him when it came to selecting the squad for the previous Lions tour. It didn't help that Rory had his critics in the press, people who were quick to point out his deficiencies. So when he first met Joe, he was a little anxious, and blurted out that he was working on his fitness and on his ball-carrying.

Joe completely disarmed Rory with his reply. He told him that while it was good that he was working on this skill, that was not actually what he wanted from him.

'The Ireland side I am going to build will have enough ball-carriers. Instead I want you to hit rucks. If you can hit thirty rucks for us in a game and don't carry the ball once but we get quick ball and get some of our big backs or back rows onto it, that will be enough for me.'[1]

The thing about hitting rucks is that it's kind of invisible. Most people, even fans, don't see it, and they certainly don't see it as being as good as running 30 metres to score a try. Hitting rucks makes other people look good.

Joe said: 'If you do that for me, I will see it. Trust me. I will see it, even if others don't.'[2]

In one sentence, Joe went right to the heart of Rory's inse-curity: *the fact that his value was not obvious to everyone*. By telling Rory that *he* saw it, that *he* saw the vital role the Ulsterman played in the team, he transformed Rory's confidence, and thereby his game.

'As a result of that one conversation, I would go on to play some of the best rugby of my life.'

What did that conversation generate?

Trust.

The great thing about trust is that it tends to be recipro-cated. If you believe that I trust you, you'll tend to trust me. Rory had already seen clear evidence of how game-smart Joe was. With the addition of that level of trust, captain and coach were primed to deliver as they never had before.

'I had absolute trust in him,' says Rory. 'I always believed in what Joe was doing, and that he was right, and that's why our relationship was so good, and that's ultimately why we were successful.'

We can approach leadership from a variety of angles, but no matter how we come to it, we continually find ourselves talking about trust. Time and again, I've seen how it draws out the very best in people and allows them to achieve aston-ishing things.

Silo Destruction

In Chapter 9: *Creative Thinking,* I talked about how my friend and colleague Michael Dempsey helped to dramatically improve cancer care in Ireland by breaking down the silos that had sprung up between surgeons, oncologists, radiologists and GPs. It's a remarkable thing, how easy it is for cliques to develop in any given situation. And there are few things more damaging to innovation and performance than cliques. Why? Because once a clique forms, all principles, values and goals slip into second place behind doing what's best to keep the clique alive. Collaboration is all about introducing trust into the equation, showing those within silos that they have nothing to fear and everything to gain by breaking down those barriers.

> There are few things more damaging to innovation and performance than cliques

We talked earlier, too, about our collaboration with Lidl Ireland in transforming an underperforming company culture. At the time, sales growth was stagnant and an internal survey indicated that management no longer trusted the board.

Where there's mistrust, you'll always find two things: bad communication and cliques. In that regard, Lidl was no different. Operations, property, buying, admin, finance and HR worked side by side, but separately, concentrating on their own deliverables. This created both over-communication and under-communication.

Then-COO Martin Bailee explains: 'If you needed someone to do something, you cc'd their boss and their boss's boss, and the reply to the mail cc'd half a dozen more. It was a blame game. The culture of mistrust evident in that internal survey was apparent throughout the organisation.'

Just to give one example of the many ways in which siloing was damaging the business: at the time, the company was opening between ten and twenty stores a year. That process pulled in many different departments, each of which had its own timelines.

'So suppose you get really bad weather and can't build for two weeks. In a silo'd organisation, everyone else carries on regardless. Staff are hired and trained, giving you additional costs. More particularly, you're not managing the expectations of new recruits, who are supposed to be ambassadors in the community. The organisation's attitude of "Just get it done regardless" – sure, you always need an element of that; after all, it's what had delivered time and again – but the lack of joined-up thinking was now putting a brake on that growth. What we needed was: "Just get it done, but in a smarter, more sustainable, more efficient way."'

The process begun in the aftermath of that damning trust index score saw the company establish a set of shared values, and little by little, as management began to buy-in to those values, behaviours began to shift. The blame culture, with its endless cc'ing, ended, and in place, communication – real communication – began to ramp up.

Not Coin-operated

The research has shown us time and again that working in interconnected teams is how millennials (or Generation Y) and the generation coming behind them – centennials – like to work.

'The younger generations want to work *with* you, not *for* you,' says psychologist and coach Dr Mary Collins. 'They respond to transformational leadership so much better than the old command-and-control-style leadership. If you want to get the best from a young workforce, you need to take a transformational approach.'

Today's workers are not coin-operated.

'Generation Y are certainly a different generation from those past,' says Mary. 'For companies looking to attract Generation-Y talent, they need to ensure their employer-value proposition fits in with the needs and values of this rising proportion of the talent pool. Attracting them early, retaining them by meeting their mobility, flexibility and continuous feedback demands, and communicating an employee-value proposition that appeals to their desire for collaboration, contribution and global altruism are key if employers wish to vie successfully for their attention.'[3]

These issues are not restricted to the corporate environment. I've mentioned my college football coach, Dessie Ryan, before. Another Level 5 leader, he understood the value of giving his teams autonomy long before this idea took root in boardrooms and C-suites.

Twenty-five years ago, we made it through to the finals of the Sigerson Cup Gaelic football competition. We'd been trying to win it without success for the previous five years. Myself and many of my colleagues on the team were in our final year, so this was our last chance. Dessie had asked seven of the leaders on that team – of which I was one – to meet him in the pavilion in Queen's University the week before the finals. We thought he'd be telling us who would be in the squad that would travel to the tournament in Galway, but Dessie had a surprise for us.

'*You* are going to pick the final squad,' he told us. 'Anyone you feel should not be on the bus, they're not going to be on the bus. You pick the squad, and give me a call later to let me know who's in it.'

I don't think Dessie could have come up with a more empowering initiative. We picked the squad, and a week later we travelled south for the tournament. We made it through to the final, and in driving rain that Sunday, we finally secured the title.

Adversarial Collaboration

Adversarial collaboration is an idea developed by Nobel laureate Daniel Kahneman, author of the highly influential *Thinking, Fast and Slow*. It works like this: two people with opposing views work together to evolve a position that satisfies both.

In the world of academia, hostility between scholars with opposing views can be pretty toxic. I've found too that when this kind of conflict occurs, it only serves to strengthen views on either side and widen the distance between them. If someone viciously denounces something you believe true, you start to identify with your view, and cling ever more tightly to it, even if new information undermines it.

In the early 2000s, Kahneman found himself in strong disagreement with another eminent psychologist, Gary Klein, on the subject of intuitive decision making. Instead of going in search of evidence to back up what he believed, he invited Klein to work with him to try to resolve the dissonance in their views.

In a 2015 interview, he told the *Guardian*: 'We spent five or six years trying to figure out the boundary, where he's right, where I am right. And that was a very satisfying experience. We wrote a paper entitled "A Failure to Disagree".'[4]

In our organisation, the culture is one of continual challenge. I need people to stand up and tell me when they think I'm wrong. Time and again, I've found that the best way forward is through challenge and respectful argument.

The Eight Collaboration Success Factors

A 2007 study by Lynda Gratton of the London Business School and author Tamara J. Erickson took a deep dive into what makes large collaborative teams work. They isolated eight success factors.[5]

1. Great leadership is vital: 'Teams do well when executives invest in supporting social relationships, demonstrate collaborative behaviour themselves, and create what we call a "gift culture" – one in which employees experience interactions with leaders and colleagues as something valuable and generously offered, a gift.'[6]

2. Social relationships. The most successful collaborations happened in companies where the executives set a lot of store by encouraging great relationships across the company. In particular, these exemplars had what Gratton and Erickson called 'signature' practices – in other words, they did things that were both memorable and difficult for others to replicate. For example, when Royal Bank

of Scotland opened a new HQ in 2005, the campus was designed like a small town, in which the 3,000 employees rubbed shoulders with each other every day.[7]

3. Leader behaviour. If employees saw senior leaders co-operating, this positive behaviour tended to cascade down through the organisation. In Standard Chartered, for example, long-standing collaborations between members of the general management committee allowed them to easily substitute for one another when someone was absent. When employees see this kind of thing happening at the top table, they tend to emulate it.

4. Mentoring, both formal and informal, played a big role in companies that boasted the best collaborations.

5. Skills are crucial. Even if you've got a collaborative culture, you won't see successful collaboration unless HR invests in training team members in things like purposeful communication, conflict resolution and project management.

6. Team leadership. The best teams had leaders who were both task- and relationship-oriented. In other words, the ability to make objectives and responsibilities clear, and to provide monitoring and feedback, were as important as the softer skills: developing trust and goodwill between team members.

7. Establish teams in which some members already know each other. The researchers found that in new teams, where everyone is a stranger to everyone else, it can take a lot of time for trust to be established. Sprinkle the team

with those who already have good relationships with each other and the process is fast-tracked. One caveat: you've got to ensure that those with prior knowledge of each other don't hive off into a subgroup but instead draw everyone into the circle.

8. Make sure every member of the team has a clear understanding of their role within the group. This is more important than clarity around *how* the goal will be reached. If there's role ambiguity, time and energy is burned negotiating turf and jostling for status. By contrast, if everyone knows what they're there for, that time goes into figuring out the best way forward.

Collaborating in a Crisis

I like the simplicity and power of Bernard Byrne's definition of leadership: 'It's about creating an environment where everyone can deliver at their best.'

When he joined AIB Bank as CFO in 2010, the organisation was still reeling from the global financial crisis. He points out that when you step into the middle of a crisis, what you really need isn't leadership so much as management. You need triage. You need to figure out what needs to be done – fast – and then be directive and unambiguous about the action that must be taken.

Here, the leader-as-manager needs two things. Self-awareness and situational awareness.

Bernard says, 'As you live and grow as a leader, you –

hopefully – become a bit more self-aware. You learn from what you did wrong in the past and you learn how your actions are perceived.'

It doesn't matter if your intention is good if those who you need to collaborate with don't see that good intention. So you must be sufficiently self-aware to modulate what you say and do to take account of that. If you want people to open up to you, to be available for you, to respond well to what you ask them to do, you need to be aware of how you are with people.

Then there's situational awareness.

'Every situation is different,' says Bernard. 'The things that matter in one situation will be different to things that matter in another. Context is crucial. It determines whether one style or another is important.'

So you pause before acting. You look at yourself and then you look at the situation you're in and try to figure out as much as you can about it as quickly as possible. Bernard cites that quote, usually attributed to Einstein: 'If I had only one hour to save the world, I would spend fifty-five minutes defining the problem, and only five minutes finding the solution.'

Then, once you have worked out a plan, you draw everyone in and explain that in order to get out of crisis mode, we have to prioritise. What are the three things or the four things or the five things that need to be done?

You pause before acting. You look at yourself and then you look at the situation you're in and try to figure out as much as you can about it as quickly as possible

Here's the critical thing: if all of those priorities fall between one or two areas of operation, that doesn't mean that everyone else sits in the wings until things get better.

'You say, "For the next year, *this* is what's going to dominate our lives, so we are going to spread the workload." Now you put an organisational structure in place to make sure that everyone has one important thing they need to do, which is driven by the collective need to concentrate exclusively on these priorities. You don't just ask one person, no matter how good they are, to take on all those things.'

And it doesn't matter what people were doing pre-crisis. In order to get through this, it's all hands to the pump. You figure out a structure, and you spread the workload.

Bernard explains that when he took over as CFO in 2010, the big issue for banks was liquidity. The Irish banking system lost close to €100 billion of liquidity at that time. Confidence was so damaged and economic activity so low that no one was opening new deposit or current accounts. Regaining that liquidity was the first priority.

The second priority related to SME lending: how could the bank continue to support small businesses?

The third priority was mortgages. In the aftermath of the property collapse, large numbers of borrowers were struggling with repayments.

'I let everyone know that these were the three issues, and together, we set up a structure to ensure that these were the *only* things that would be dealt with as priorities. People used to come to me with ideas for increasing profitability here or improving things there. I had to tell them, "Listen, if what you're suggesting doesn't move one of these three issues, we're not talking about it. We're not devoting resources, we're not giving you any extra money. If it's not about these three issues, I can't focus on it now."'

These were tough calls. Those whose areas were not prioritised felt excluded and a little demotivated. There are consequences for refusing to accept someone else's priority. Constant communication, reminding everyone why these priorities mattered so much, was crucial to maintaining morale.

Here again is where that self-awareness piece comes in. You need to ensure that you have the support structures around you to help you deal with making these tough calls.

Structural rigidity can be a big problem in these crisis situations. Large organisations cling to their hierarchies and systems. In an emergency, they become a maze that firefighters have to navigate to get to the blaze. The people who can solve the crisis are frequently present in the organisation already. The leader just has to find a way to get them where they need to be, *then* get them working together.

And there's one element that researchers have isolated as being of vital importance in helping people to work well together: psychological safety. The reassurance that it's OK to be human, it's OK to make mistakes.

In Summary

- Trust is essential to great collaboration.
- Silos are a barrier to collaboration. Break them down.
- Remember, Generation Y wants to work with you, not for you!
- Surprise your team by empowering them to make big decisions.
- Adversarial collaboration can ignite innovation and ultimately deliver massively for your organisation.
- Collaboration in a crisis is essential.

CHAPTER 13:
PSYCHOLOGICAL SAFETY
It's OK to Be Human

On 29 October 2018, Lion Air flight 610 crashed into the Java Sea thirteen minutes after take-off, killing all 189 passengers and crew. The plane, a Boeing 737 MAX, was new, and had only been introduced by Lion Air – an Indonesian airline – the previous year. The investigation into the causes of the crash revealed a range of technical issues, including a design flaw in the automated flight control system, or MCAS. This system was supposed to compensate for the heavier engines in this series of planes by automatically adjusting the nose of the plane to prevent stalling. The problem, it would emerge, was that MCAS engaged shortly after take-off, and the pilots could not regain control of the aircraft when it began to nosedive. The accident prompted Boeing to issue warnings and training advisories to any airline operating a MAX series plane. And yet, a little over five months later, another Boeing 737 MAX crashed, this one in Ethiopia. As in Indonesia, there were no survivors. In the aftermath of this disaster, all MAX series planes were grounded.

Again, the investigation zeroed in on technical issues and in particular the MCAS system, but in the months that followed, it became clear that it wasn't that simple. In December 2019, Boeing handed over a file of internal employee messages to a US congressional enquiry into the Boeing 737 Max. When this file was published a month later, it revealed a great deal about the culture at the aircraft manufacturer.

In a message sent in April 2017, eighteen months before the first crash, an employee complained about the MAX's flight management technology. They wrote: 'This airplane is designed by clowns who in turn are supervised by monkeys.'[1] They also talked about the plane's 'piss-poor design' and said, 'I'll be shocked if the FAA (Federal Aviation Authority) passes this turd.'[2]

In a 2018 message, an employee said, 'I still haven't been forgiven by God for the covering up I did last year.'[3]

Peter DeFazio, chair of the US House Committee on Transportation and Infrastructure, described the messages as outrageous.

'This is not about one employee,' he said, 'this is about a failure of a safety culture at Boeing in which undue pressure is placed on employees to meet deadlines and ensure profitability at the expense of safety. Boeing will have to answer for this ...'[4]

An investigation into a Boeing factory in South Carolina by the *New York Times* found that employees were penalised for drawing attention to defects and substandard practices.

In his book *Sooner, Safer, Happier*, business writer Jonathan Smart points out that according to that same Times investigation, several former employees alleged that managers pushed quality inspectors to stop recording defects. Some employees were actually fired when they voiced concerns. More than a dozen safety complaints were filed with federal regulators, some of which detailed this pressure to not report violations.[5]

In its final report published in September 2020, the US House Transportation and Infrastructure Committee said: 'The MAX crashes were ... a horrific culmination of a series of faulty technical assumptions by Boeing's engineers, a lack of transparency on the part of Boeing's management and grossly insufficient oversight by the FAA.'[6]

This was an organisational culture wholly lacking in psychological safety.

When people are afraid to speak up, to criticise management or draw attention to defects and problems, you have an organisation where, at the very least, there will be no innovation. And at worst, people will die.

The best and most complete definition

This was an organisational culture wholly lacking in psychological safety

of psychological safety comes from Harvard professor Amy Edmondson. It is 'the assurance that one can speak up, offer ideas, point out problems, or deliver bad news without fear of retribution.'[7]

When something catastrophic happens, it's hard to bypass hindsight. You think, 'In that situation, I'd have done something about it. I'd have gone to the top or gone to the media. People's lives were at risk.'

The reality, however, is that most of the time, people don't come forward. There are two reasons for this. The first is obvious. Breaking ranks with your colleagues, standing up and speaking the truth to those in power is exceptionally difficult. Whistle-blowers are almost always disbelieved. They're frequently silenced and often vilified. If you know that making a stand will have a serious negative impact on your life and the lives of those you love, it's going to be very easy to talk yourself out of it.

The other reason why we don't tend to come forward is because of a psychological phenomenon called 'discounting the future'. We tell ourselves that the bad thing might never happen. The possibility of disaster is only relevant to some vague and distant future. But standing up and saying, 'Hang on, this is wrong,' that happens in the present, the here and now, and is far more difficult to discount.

Amy Edmondson puts it like this: 'It's simple human nature. We don't want to ruffle feathers ... We don't want to be thought of as stupid when we say: "I just don't see how this is going to work." We don't want a dressing-down when we point out a quality problem.'[8]

Ego

If Boeing demonstrated how not to do it, Alan Mulally – a former vice president at Boeing – demonstrated how to get it right. Mulally is credited with turning around the fortunes of the Ford Motor Company after he took over as CEO in 2006. His recovery plan makes for fascinating reading, but right now I want to talk about the weekly business-plan review meetings that he instigated with senior staff very soon after he took over. At the first of these, each executive was asked to deliver status reports on progress towards company goals. Mulally stopped the meeting halfway through and pointed out that despite the fact that the company was in line to lose billions of dollars that year, everyone was reporting positively. Every single executive projected growth in their area.

'Why is every line green?' he asked. 'Isn't there anything that's not going well here?'[9]

At the second of these business-plan reviews, one executive – Mark Fields – took his courage in his hands and told the truth. Fields was head of the division that was about to introduce the Ford Edge. A grinding noise had been reported from the suspension, and it looked as though this would delay the launch. The company was approaching the end of the year, a time when everyone is under pressure to achieve sales targets. The temptation to bury the problem must have been immense. But Fields stuck to his guns and explained the issue. His accompanying slide showed not a green but a red line. When he sat down at the end of his presentation, the room fell silent. His colleagues must have thought that he was about to be fired, but to everyone's surprise, Mulally started clapping.

'Mark,' he said, 'that's great visibility. Who can help Mark with this?'[10]

The following week, in the third meeting, there was no shortage of red lines in every presentation. Now, everything was out in the open. Now, Mulally could put the processes in place to begin turning the ship around.

The point is that if people do not want to give you bad news, that's your fault, not theirs. In Chapter 6: *No Ego* we talked about the dangers of being overly focused on your own ego. If you're hung up on your status, you're going to end up surrounded by sycophants and yes-men. You'll be insecure and easy to manipulate. Bill Walsh knew this. He's a legend in American football. During his time as head coach to the San Francisco 49ers, the team won three National Football Conference (NFC) championships and three Super Bowls. In 1993 he gave a wide-ranging interview to the *Harvard Business Review*, in which he was asked what was the biggest obstacle to creating a successful team.

If people do not want to give you bad news, that's your fault, not theirs

Walsh said that people must be able to communicate without fear. They have to believe that they won't be ridiculed if they turn out to be wrong, or if their views don't line up with those of the coach. 'That is where the breakthrough comes. That is what it takes to build a successful, winning organisation.'[11]

Google Teams

In 2013, Google researchers set out to find exactly what made a great team great. Over a two-year period, they conducted over 200 interviews with over 180 active teams, expecting to find some kind of formula: a great team needs two of *this* kind of person, three of *that* kind of person and so on. What they found, however, was that the make-up of the team wasn't half as important as how the team members interacted, how they structured their work and viewed each other's contributions. They discovered five key dynamics that set successful teams apart. First and foremost? Psychological safety: 'Can we take risks on this team without feeling insecure or embarrassed?'

For the record, the other four were dependability (members get things done on time and to a high standard), structure and clarity (clear roles, plans and goals), meaning (the work means something to members) and impact (members believe their work creates change).

Julia Rozovsky, an analyst at Google People Operations, said the research found that psychological safety was 'far and away' the most important of these five dynamics.

'It's the underpinning of the other four. How could that be? Taking a risk around your team members seems simple. But remember the last time you were working on a project. Did you feel like you could ask what the goal was without the risk of sounding like you're the only one out of the loop? Or did you opt for continuing without clarifying anything, in order to avoid being perceived as someone who is unaware?'[12]

It's very difficult to embed psychological safety in a culture that lacks it. You can't just say, 'Right, we're going to do psychological safety from now on.' It's more about creating the environment in which it can emerge naturally. We talked in Chapter 7: *Empathy*, about how inspirational leadership comes through establishing a nurturing environment: building connection, creating the conditions for mutual trust. It's the same with psychological safety. Someone who feels trusted and who trusts the leader is not going to be afraid to ask questions, point out problems or suggest bold new directions of travel. Remember too that you won't harness the power of a diverse team unless everyone is given the space to contribute authentically.

And it comes back again to purpose, to that big 'Why'. If your team is united by a shared vision of creating something meaningful, that's the thing that gets them to work in the morning, and that's the thing that they'll fight to hold onto. A great purpose makes people fearless.

In Summary

- Psychological safety is the assurance that you can speak up, offer ideas or deliver bad news without fear of retribution.

- A lack of psychological safety at Boeing killed 346 people. What is psychological safety like in your organisation?

- If you're new to your organisation, make it clear that you welcome the truth, no matter how bad it may be.

- Psychological safety isn't a nice-to-have, it's the most essential ingredient in creating a successful team.

CHAPTER 14:

CULTURE

Culture Eats Strategy for Breakfast, Lunch and Dinner

In the months coming up to the Russia World Cup of 2018, few teams were more closely scrutinised, discussed and fretted over than England. A nation starved of footballing success had become used to seeing the national side routinely underperform on the world stage. Just two years earlier England had been dumped out of the Euro 2016 tournament by Iceland, a team of semi-professionals managed by a dentist.

In the end, Gareth Southgate – a relatively untested manager – brought the youngest team in the tournament to within thirty minutes of a World Cup final, and to their first semifinal appearance in twenty-eight years. Now, there's little doubt that luck played a role in the team's success. Luck will play a role in every human endeavour. But the truth is that the achievements of Southgate and his squad were meticulously planned and expertly executed. This was no fluke.

To understand where this success came from, you have to go back to 2014, four years before the World Cup, when the English FA announced the beginning of something they called 'England DNA'. It would be 'the starting point for the creation of a world-class culture of elite player development that leads to winning England teams'.[1]

There were several elements to this new approach, but continuity would be key. The FA aimed to create a 'golden thread' linking youth teams and the senior team. Gareth Southgate was manager of the England U21 squad at the time. In an interview with the *Guardian* newspaper at the launch, he pointed out that the German players who had won the World Cup the previous summer had an average of twenty youth caps more than their English counterparts by the time they reached their senior teams; the implication being that the German players had a great deal more exposure to and experience of the culture and ethos of the international set-up before they graduated to the senior squad.[2]

The two years following the announcement of the England DNA cultural blueprint were not good ones for English football, however. Managerial difficulties followed the humiliating exit from Euro 2016. Roy Hodgson departed the job at this point and his successor, Sam Allardyce, lasted only sixty-seven days. There's no doubt that few top-flight managers were banging down the FA's door looking for a chance to manage the national side. It is among the most pressurised positions in professional sport; every decision you make is the subject of forensic examination by what can often be a vicious media. When Southgate was finally appointed after a spell as interim manager, both press and fans greeted the decision with alarm. The *Daily Mirror* reported that Twitter reacted with 'a mass wail of despair' at Southgate's appointment.[3] The BBC pointed out that Southgate's club record was the worst of any manager of the past twenty years, then quoted a string of football writers, all of whom were underwhelmed by the new appointment.[4] Nobody pointed out that if the FA was serious about the England DNA project, Gareth Southgate – a man steeped in that culture – was the logical candidate.

Once appointed, Southgate set about establishing a back-room team who shared both his and the FA's vision for the future of English football. Assistant manager Steve Holland was appointed in the summer preceding the 2018 World Cup, together with a large team of analysis and performance specialists, and crucially, a sports psychologist who would work with coaches and players to embed a degree of resilience in the squad.

Preparation, Preparation, Preparation

Let's go back for a minute to that England DNA launch in 2014. Then FA Director Dan Ashworth stated that a key element of the culture on the pitch would be 'tactical flexibility'.[5] The new approach would not marry the team to any particular formation, but would prepare them both to dominate the middle of the pitch and be capable of adapting to whatever strategic combination the opposition threw at them. In the eighteen matches under Southgate's leadership ahead of the World Cup, he experimented with a variety of formations and a variety of players, seeking out a tactical approach that optimised his resources while at the same time preserving the capacity to adapt to changes and new threats as they arose. In an interview with the London *Independent* in advance of the squad's departure for Russia, Southgate said, 'We have to have some consistency in formation, some consistency in what we are asking the players to do. We have to focus on a system and really try to hone it, to work on it, improve it, and that might mean that we might have to leave some good players out.'[6]

The key thing here is that the status, the stardom of individual players, would be subservient to the system. The message here is clear: this would not be a squad based around individual brilliance. Instead, it would be composed of individuals signed up to a unified vision. There would be a unity of purpose.

As July approached, it was interesting to see the narrative about the team shift in the press. The despair and bewilderment that had greeted Southgate's appointment had given way to a grudging optimism. The eighteen games Southgate had overseen since his appointment had not been especially good. Ten wins, two losses and six draws – and no major scalp among those ten victories. But the team had qualified comfortably, and one word surfaced continually in press reports. Cohesion. The sense was emerging that this was a team fully subscribed to a common purpose. We were beginning to see the results of all the work that was being done.

It's also very instructive to see how Southgate and the squad communicated with press and fans. First of all, he was *open*. Southgate did not run from the hard truths. He frequently acknowledged that England had won a meagre three knock-out games in major tournaments in the previous twenty-five years, compared to twenty-three in Germany. Secondly, Southgate made it abundantly clear that this England team was not the finished product. It was a work in progress. The 2018 World Cup was not the destination, merely a station on the way. Southgate and co. very skilfully mitigated the burgeoning national anxiety that the national team tends to generate in the approach to a big competition. By naming a young squad (the most inexperienced in age and caps in the competition), not only was there greater scope to draw them towards that aforementioned unity of purpose, it also served to lighten the terrible weight of expectation that had crippled successive England teams.

Reports from inside the camp made much of how relaxed the team was. At training sessions in Repino, where the team was based, fans watched images of the players mucking about and having fun. This may seem insignificant. It isn't.

One thing that I have witnessed time and again among both the sports and corporate teams with whom I have worked is that fun is a vital ingredient of success. When I worked with Leinster rugby, if someone came in late, a chant would go up: 'Roll the dice! Roll the dice!' The dice would come out, and depending on which number came up, the latecomer would have to do a hundred jumping jacks, or sing a song in front of the group. Fun breaks up tension, it allows a team to gel.

A team that works well together is one that performs when the chips are down. A team that breaks down tensions and inhibitions with fun and games always does a much better job of harnessing the talents and creativity of individual members.

Also, how does seeing players having fun impact on press and fans? It communicates the fact that players are not wound up, they're not over-thinking the game. We also saw footage of players playing darts with the press. Again, you're showing a relaxed team, but as well as that, it's that bit harder to write something critical about a footballer if you've been playing darts with him the night before. So, in place of the fevered atmosphere that usually permeates an England entourage, you had a sense of a team comfortable in its own skin, a team with nothing to hide, a team ready to slip easily into the flow state when time came to perform.

Interviewed before the quarter-final against Colombia – a stage at which most England teams had crumbled in the past – Southgate said that this was a brilliant opportunity to go beyond where most teams have gone before. 'The lads have got a chance to write their own stories,' he told the press. Again, he was breaking out of the straitjacket of the past. In that same interview, he told talkSPORT, 'If anything, we should feel freer. It is a game we are really looking forward to, the sort of match you want to be involved in. It is going to be a fantastic evening.'[7]

Remember, this was on the threshold of the first knock-out game the team faced – the very obstacle that had destroyed England teams for twenty years, the one around which the anxiety of a nation gravitated like a black hole. Where was the fear? *It's going to be a fantastic evening.* Southgate should have been quaking in his waistcoat, but instead he was looking forward to the game. Again, he was making it clear that this was not the England of old. Things had changed. The culture had been redrafted. As he says, the team was writing its own story.

Leadership Style

The stereotypical view of the team manager is the loud, bullish alpha male driving his team forward with an iron will. Southgate doesn't conform to that stereotype. He is softly spoken. His side-line demeanour is calm. Watching him mingle with players before extra time against Croatia, on the brink of a World Cup final, he was focused but calm – issuing individual instructions instead of a bombastic rabble-rousing war cry. In fact, throughout that match, Southgate was anonymous. As his opposite number Zlatko Dalić was in constant motion on the side-line, Southgate stood calmly watching. Even when England took the lead after five minutes, while staff and substitutes (and the entire English population) leaped up in celebration, he remained dignified, focused and unruffled. A report in the *Telegraph* after that match said, 'You could never mistake Southgate's low profile with any lack of personality, passion or desire, and if ever there was a football manager who became an overnight hero after decades of diligent, unseen work, it's him.'[8]

Similarly, don't mistake a passive demeanour for some kind of nice-guy pushover. In the two years between that embarrassing knockout against Iceland and the first game of the World Cup against Tunisia, Southgate oversaw a complete clean-out of the English squad. In choosing who would go to Russia, he passed over several superstars in order to create the squad he wanted, making decisions that were characterised as ruthless in some quarters. Long-term goalkeeper Joe Hart was omitted in favour of three less experienced options – Jack Butland, Nick Pope and Jordan Pickford. All three had put in very strong performances in the Premier League ahead of the competition, so they were chosen over Hart. It was youth over experience, performance over pedigree.

Witness, too, the demeanour of the squad when faced with adversity. When goals were conceded – as against Colombia – there was no panic, either from Southgate or from his players. They did not crumble, they remained focused on maintaining their performance.

Culture Is Catching

Creating unity of purpose in a squad of twenty-three players is an obvious challenge. To do so in an organisation of hundreds or even thousands of people is even more difficult, but watching how the culture established in the English squad broke beyond those narrow confines demonstrates how a strong, positive culture can become embedded on a much broader basis. Articles appeared, not in the sports pages but in the colour sections of the British press, talking about Southgate as a 'symbol of positive masculinity'. Much was made of the fact that he encouraged squad member Fabian Delph to return home to be with his wife, who was due to give birth. Southgate was quoted as saying, 'Some things in life are more important than football ... It is about a bit of perspective in life.'⁹

In the aftermath of England's victory over Colombia, Southgate was seen not celebrating with the squad but commiserating with the Colombian player who had missed the penalty. And conversely, after England were eventually defeated by Croatia in the semi-final, Southgate waited on the pitch until the celebrations had abated, then went round and congratulated each and every Croatian player.

Instead of seeking stories about past indiscretions, the press began digging up stories about what a good person Southgate was. While some of it may have been a little over the top, the point I'm trying to make is that a positive, open, genuine culture, where leaders are seen to walk the walk and talk the talk, takes on a life of its own. It seeps down through the organisation and recruits everyone to its cause.

If you're the leader, you cast a long shadow. People watch you. They take their cue from you.

> A positive, open, genuine culture, where leaders are seen to walk the walk and talk the talk, takes on a life of its own

Making Change Stick

It doesn't matter the performance crucible – business, sport, politics, the voluntary sector, the arts sector – cultural transformation is exceptionally difficult. It takes time and single-minded determination to turn the ship around. But sometimes, it has to be done. There's no shortage of research that confirms the value of a strong, people-oriented organisational culture. It's a vital retention tool. A recent report from Breathe HR in the UK estimated that toxic workplace culture cost the economy £20.2 billion (€23.4 billion) a year, and that 27 per cent of employees quit due to a poor company culture.[10]

I want to return again to the process of cultural transformation in Lidl.

The retailer faced two basic issues. The executive team no longer trusted the board, and the company was underperforming relative to its biggest competitor, Aldi.

Determining exactly how the company would institute change didn't happen overnight. The board and the leadership team began with a series of offsite sessions at which vision, mission, employee value proposition, brand value proposition and core values were thoroughly explored. They asked themselves what it meant to be a values-driven organisation. They'd always been a value-driven organisation, but 'values-driven'? What did that even mean? At the end of this lengthy process, they settled on four values, which they agreed to try to embed in the organisation: trust, respect, recognition and responsibility. Both leadership team and board went into considerable detail on what each of these terms meant.

'The crux question,' says Martin Bailee, then COO of the company, 'the single departure point from which everything else would follow, was simply this: who are we, and who should we be? The point is that these values had to be so embedded in what we did, they had to be so natural to us, that we should not have to have this moment again.

'Because our executive team had told us they didn't trust us, and because of the ways in which that lack of trust was hampering the business, those values would have to cascade from the top down. But widen out that perspective and you can see, actually *everyone told us they didn't trust us*. We weren't the preferred shop; we were lagging our key competitor in market share. This told us that change would also have to happen from the bottom up. The CEO must live by the new values, but so must those on the till. For the first time, Lidl would become customer-centric, and in that I am referring to both the company's internal and actual customer.'

At this point, neither those working on the shop floor, nor indeed any of the management layers up to and including area managers, had any awareness of the process that the leadership team were engaged in. Why? Because they had to get it right at the top first. Change would only be sustainable if the exec team became ambassadors for that change. Begin the process of cascading down too soon and it would not be credible. It would go off half-cocked and only succeed in deepening the mistrust.

That process of full engagement between executive team and the board continued for six months. They discussed how these agreed values would be embedded in everything that they did. The company introduced KBIs – key behavioural indicators – into the mix and required the executive team to live the new culture with the same diligence that they applied themselves to the key performance indicators (KPIs).

'Over those first six months, it was possible to see the slow transformation of sceptics into adopters,' says Martin.

'It also became apparent who were the people who were writing themselves out of the picture, those who weren't managing the KPIs sustainably, who weren't managing KBIs at all, who were reverting to type. It wasn't hard to spot the difference between those who had adopted the new growth mindset and those who remained stuck in the old, fixed way of thinking.'

The acid test of this change was in how everyone behaved when the pressure came on. In this respect, the executive team policed themselves. When there were team members who could not transition, it was not the board that identified the exception, it was the leadership team who said – in so many words – this person should not be with us.

'So it was a very poignant moment when the team came to us six months into the project and said, "OK, we're ready. We're ready to take this and run with it."'

At this point, the leadership team took the values that they had been living for the previous six months and brought them to the area managers.

The HR team used the Hartman Profiling technique to better understand the personalities of its internal leaders. This is a relatively simple tool, which uses a questionnaire and a four-colour scheme to classify how people are motivated: red by power, blue by intimacy, white by peace and yellow by fun.

'This process', says Martin, 'allowed us to see which leaders were compatible with which. You wouldn't believe how much that helped to resolve conflicts.'

As the process of transformation progressed, there were many, many challenges.

'We sometimes found, particularly in the early stages, that the values were being flung back at us. Suppose someone failed to deliver on a deadline and you needed to have a stern conversation. Sometimes we got, 'So much for trust and respect. I'm sat here in a disciplinary process ...' Of course, the reality is that this conversation was entirely consistent with the values – I'm citing "responsibility" here – because the manager had failed to deliver. There's no ambiguity. This is why self-policing became so important. Just because we're talking about values doesn't mean we've become all touchy-feely. We're still running a business. Those behavioural issues arose frequently as the transformation cascaded down through the managerial levels. The message we had to deliver was this: we're not asking you to stop doing your job, we're asking you to do it better. This is how we're going to help.'

It was a further three months before area managers were ready to begin introducing the now-entrenched values to those below them in the hierarchy. And here, perhaps, is the most pleasing thing about the whole process. To recap, it took six months for the leadership team of sixty-four executives to buy in to the process. Six months of witnessing the board walking the walk as well as talking the talk proved to them that they were serious about this change. There would be no backsliding, no reverting to type when the pressure came on. So by the time the area managers were formally introduced to the new

> 'The message we had to deliver was this: we're not asking you to stop doing your job, we're asking you to do it better'

culture, they had already been witnessing the leadership team living and breathing it for the previous six months. They had seen change, positivity and new behaviours; they had seen leadership through coaching rather than the usual management through pressure.

'This is why it only took half the time for our area managers to become sufficiently bought in to be able to introduce the new dispensation to the remaining 4,500 employees. So we had a snowball effect. All of this positive change cascaded down through the organisation with far greater speed than I would have thought possible. Those 4,500 employees were seeing, for the first time, clear alignment between purpose, practice and performance.'

A range of innovations were introduced. Technological solutions were found to help reduce paperwork and condense processes to free up capacity, to the point where the company was able to reduce contracted management hours by three a week. This enabled more family-friendly working arrangements. Health and wellbeing became a cornerstone of HR. You could see the impact of that almost as soon as it was introduced, with people going for runs at lunchtime. Streamlined communications up and down the organisation (which included a corporate magazine, which surprised everyone with how popular it became) helped to create a unity of purpose.

'By the time I moved to Lidl UK, Lidl Ireland was unrecognisable,' says Martin. 'And this process became, in time, a blueprint for change across the group. The retail world underwent something of a revolution during those four years, and yet we managed to reverse our position vis-à-vis our key competitor, securing a 1-per-cent market-share advantage over Aldi. That move, from minus one to plus one, is without doubt the most accurate gauge of the impact of cultural transformation on Lidl. Both discounters were subject to the same external factors, but only Lidl underwent profound change. We adopted a values-driven culture, one that enabled us to become a best-in-class, customer-centric retailer with a more dynamic offering of Irish, regional and international products. We made one of the leanest operating models in the world even leaner, underpinned by a set of KBIs, which put all of this change on a sustainable footing.'

Later, when Lidl International rejuvenated its own vision and mission statement – and introduced corporate values for the first time – Lidl Ireland's transformation experience in essence became a supportive blueprint for the group.

Leadership is not about making popular choices, it's about convincing people to take a difficult path towards a better place. And that takes time. What Gareth Southgate discovered, as the board discovered in Lidl, is that there comes a tipping point, a snowball effect. If you sustain that fight against the old orthodoxy, change will come and it will unseat the default way of doing things, turning a vicious cycle into a virtuous one.

> Leadership is not about making popular choices, it's about convincing people to take a difficult path towards a better place

In Summary

- Culture eats strategy for breakfast, lunch and dinner, in your team, your organisation and your community.
- Sometimes it's the gentle, introverted leader that can have the greatest impact on culture.
- Great culture becomes contagious. Living the values at the top allows those values to cascade down through the organisation.
- Choose your cultural custodians wisely.
- Leadership is not about making popular choices, it's about convincing people to take a difficult path towards a better place.

CHAPTER 15:

DIFFICULT CONVERSATIONS

You Can't Achieve Excellence with Hugs Alone

Being empathetic, being optimistic, being purposeful and collaborative – none of these things mean that you run from conflict. None of these things mean you avoid difficult conversations. For leadership to be real there has to be a willingness to confront problems as they arise.

My friend and colleague Eugene Conlon talks about one of the many conflict situations he has encountered over his career.

'Financial controller. Really bright guy. He wanted to move into management. As part of his review process, we gathered feedback from those who worked along-side him. While he excelled at the technical skills required for the job, his people skills were very, very poor. Those around him felt that he didn't respect them. His style was authoritarian: *this is what we have to do and my way is the only way to do it.* Collaboration? Not his strong suit. Instead of harnessing the creativity of those he

For leadership to be real there has to be a willingness to confront problems as they arise

worked with, he would set out both the goal and the means to achieve it. This demoralises bright people, and this is what lay behind their feedback. They described him as arrogant, aloof, cold. Several said that if he was promoted to a position of authority over them, they would leave immediately. Time and again I've seen the proof of that truism: people leave managers, not organisations. And I've also seen – particularly in engineering companies – people promoted based on their technical skills without any reference to their emotional intelligence.

'This guy wasn't ready to hear the criticism. He got very angry. He maintained that his technical brilliance should have been enough to earn him promotion. I had to explain to him that his lack of skills in key areas had the potential to drive people out of the organisation. He didn't accept this at all and left the organisation himself very soon afterwards.

'I met the same guy a few years later and he asked me if I remembered the last conversation we'd had. I played it down, and said I didn't really recall, but he laughed and told me that he stayed angry at me for quite a while before eventually coming round to the idea that maybe I had a point. Maybe he did have gaps in his skills. So he went off and studied privately and got some mentoring and, at the time I met him, was successfully managing a high-performing team.'

Coaching

Katrina Steady dislikes the phrase 'you need to coach that person up'. This implies that you need to tell them what to do to improve their performance.

'That's not what coaching is. Coaching is seeing that someone has potential and helping them to realise that potential. You help them to achieve their goals. So you ask questions to coach them in the right direction.'

Katrina uses the GROW model, which was developed in the UK around forty years ago. The acronym stands for:

G: Goal – what is the endpoint?

R: Current Reality – where are we today?

O: Obstacles / Options – what's going to get in the way?

W: What will you do next? – how do we overcome those obstacles?

Katrina is keen to emphasise that the leader doesn't determine the goal here. Rather, they ask open-ended, thought-provoking, self-discovering questions. 'What is your goal? What is your end game? Let's paint the picture of how that looks for you once you've achieved it.'

Next, you explore the current reality. 'Where are you right now compared to where you need to go? What resources do you have? What resources do you lack? What are the issues you face? All of these questions seek to understand exactly where the coachee is at right now.'

Now, we know where we are and where we want to go. So you talk through obstacles, the things that stand between current reality and your goal, then you explore the options to overcome these obstacles. 'You look at what's already been tried, you look at what's held the coachee back in the past. Who else can they talk to? What are the different paths they can take to achieve their goal?'

This is not the leader laying out a path for someone to follow, it is all about the coachee discovering that path for themselves. Similarly, the final element, 'What will you do next?' also needs to come from them. The leader simply asks the questions and peels back the layers. 'What can you do to achieve the goal? What are you most motivated to take action on?'

The process doesn't end with this conversation. It's about coming back to them, being that accountability person, the one who reminds them of their ambitions and the commitments they've made to themselves.

'Last time we spoke, you had an action item around going back to school. What's happened since? Did you watch that TED Talk I sent? What did you think about it? Did you read that book? Did it help? What changes do you need to make to the plan?'

It's all about maintaining that focus and facilitating change.

We also need to improve the coaching skills of everyone on the team, so that when members are underperforming, or failing to realise their potential, or are simply exhausted, they can help each other to face and overcome these obstacles.

Addressing Underperformance

First things first. A functional organisation needs the right HR processes to make performance-tracking and reporting work. There will be regular meetings where progress towards agreed goals is reviewed and evaluated. Underperformance, when it happens, should be picked up as early as possible through this process, and when it is, it should be brought out into the open and dealt with fairly but thoroughly.

A CEO called me early yesterday morning on exactly this subject. He said that the guy who was leading his sales team was underperforming and he'd just had a difficult conversation with him.

'He just wasn't coming to me with solutions,' he said.

'Well, did you ask him to come to you with solutions?'

'Not explicitly.'

That's the thing. You've got to be explicit. Everyone needs to know exactly what's expected of them. Back to Chapter 11: *Communication*: clarity is as necessary here as anywhere else. Once you both know where the problem lies, the leader becomes coach: 'Tell me how you're going to fix it. Tell me your ideas. What can you do better? When are you going to start? What would success look like? Who are you going to involve? What's the downside to this? What's the upside? What resources will you need? How can I support you?'

Be consistent: A performance-management process won't work if it's not rigorously implemented. Don't let review meetings be knocked out of your diary by 'more important' things.

Prepare: Get your facts ready. What was expected of this person? How did they fail to meet those expectations? Where is the evidence of this underperformance? Is it accurate?

Communicate: Let them know what you want to talk about. No one should feel ambushed: 'At next week's scheduled meeting, we're going to talk about underperformance issues. I have your figures for the last ninety days; I'd ask you to come prepared as well.'

Be honest and transparent: Don't sugar-coat. Don't be brutal either. Explain how their performance is impacting organisational goals.

Stick to the facts. Don't say, 'I feel you're not applying yourself.' Say: 'You haven't met your KPIs.' Keep the emotion out of it.

Shut up and listen: Give them a voice. Let them tell you what their experience is. Give them the agency to find a way out of the situation. Are goals unrealistic? Have you failed to support them in some way?

Mentor them: Help them find a pathway to better performance. Are they overburdened? Is there a situation at home that they need help with? Is there a skills gap that training might help with?

There are also situations where underperformance never becomes anything else and the optimum solution is to help the team

Remember, good leaders will always work to ensure that when someone has to leave, they leave with their dignity intact

member exit the organisation. Remember, good leaders will always work to ensure that when someone has to leave, they leave with their dignity intact. You follow the same principles, only on this occasion, you'll be assisting them out of the organisation. If you meet denial, always fall back on the facts. 'The numbers don't lie. KPIs are still not met, despite commitments given, despite coaching, despite training and support.'

Conflict in the Workplace

We all want to work in places where there's zero tolerance of harassment or bullying. Harassment is anything that violates a person's dignity, or creates a hostile, degrading or offensive environment for that person. Characteristics relevant to harassment are age, disability, gender reassignment, race, religion or belief, sex or sexual orientation. According to the UK's Advisory Conciliation and Arbitration Service (ACAS), bullying includes 'offensive, intimidating, malicious or insulting behaviour, an abuse or misuse of power through means that undermine, humiliate, denigrate or injure the recipient'.[1]

Research by the Chartered Institute of Personnel and Development (CIPD) finds that the most common forms of bullying and harassment are things like: being undermined or humiliated in your job, persistent and unwanted criticism, unreasonable pressure about job performance, public humiliation, shouting or very heated arguments, verbal abuse and isolation or exclusion from social activities.[2]

Prevention is always better than cure, and one of the best ways of ensuring that conflict doesn't boil over into bullying or harassment is simply to know your team well. Know where they're coming from, what pressures they're subject to, what their strengths and weaknesses are. This is simply about spending time with them, working with them and coaching them over the obstacles that they're going to meet. If you know your team well, it should be possible to anticipate conflicts before they arise.

Great teams thrive on diversity, but bringing talented people with different temperaments, talents and backgrounds together will sometimes generate personality clashes and misunderstandings. Once hired, you need an excellent induction process to help the new team member to understand the culture: how you do what you do. Everybody needs to understand the values, but more especially how they're embedded in everything you do. There should be no ambiguity about what bad behaviour looks like.

As a baseline, you've got to work to make sure that everyone feels included, that everyone is supported, that their contribution is valued.

We talked before about how the best leaders stay close to the people they work with – the people they serve. From here, the leader can observe, gauge the atmosphere and intervene if intervention is necessary. Critically too, the leader needs to stay present and approachable. People have got to know that when they come to you with concerns, you will take them seriously.

These days, we want people to bring their whole selves to work. We don't want hollow work personas, we want living, breathing human beings, with their unique perspectives, experiences and quirks. We want all of the creativity and determination that they can muster. The thing is, real people can't always leave their domestic concerns at the door of the office, so you've got to be aware of the pressures that they're under, and you've got to support them when they're going through the stressful times that all of us have to go through at one time or another.

Different people respond in different ways to workplace conflict. Some react instantly, on the spur of the moment. Others may appear unaffected, but underneath a calm surface, resentment may be building. Again, know your team. Watch how they relate to each other. Regular one-on-ones with members will help to keep you in touch with how people *really* feel, so that if there are unseen tensions, you can bring them out into the open and deal with them. You don't need a formal process to prompt action. Informal conversations should be happening every day.

As discussed in the last chapter, so much comes down to how the leader behaves. So you've got to pay close attention to everything you do. There are some people on the team that you'll naturally click with, and others that you just won't. Nothing breeds resentment faster than favouritism. Ensure everyone is treated the same.

Likewise, make it clear that gossip and talking behind backs is something that you don't do and don't tolerate. That doesn't mean you close your eyes to the tension that bad behaviour might generate. Find out what's going on, and if there's a genuine issue, get it out in the open early.

Act consistently, act with integrity.

Creative Conflict

I think it's important to say, too, that there's such a thing as too much harmony in a team. Conflict is a vital source of creativity. We talked in Chapter 10 about how a lack of diversity stifles innovation. The same can be said for creative tension. The competition between John Lennon and Paul McCartney was one of the driving forces behind their astonishing productivity. To take one example, if Lennon hadn't written 'Strawberry Fields Forever', McCartney wouldn't have been spurred to write 'Penny Lane', both of which appeared on a double A-sided single in early 1967.

You find examples of competitive partnership across a variety of disciplines. Wilbur and Orville Wright squabbled for weeks about the design of the propeller for their airplane.

'After long arguments we often found ourselves in the ludicrous position of each having been converted to the other's side,' said Orville, 'with no more agreement than when the discussion began.'[3]

It was only after they had gone through this process that it dawned on them that they were both wrong, and that what they actually needed was two propellers.

The two Steves – Wozniak and Jobs – had a volatile relationship that would eventually break down, but not before they had revolutionised the computer industry. Wozniak was the computer genius, Jobs the design and marketing guru. Both sold their prize possessions – in Jobs's case a Volkswagen minibus, in Wozniak's a programmable HP calculator – to raise the $1,300 to launch their first commercial enterprise.[4]

The very best sports teams that I've worked with have been characterised by intense rivalry for starting places. The Armagh team that I played on won seven Ulster titles and one All-Ireland title, and we had ten years of high-grade internal positive competition. Sir Alex Ferguson won thirty-eight trophies in his twenty-six years with Manchester United. Fierce competition for starting places featured in all of his teams. It didn't matter how famous you were; if you weren't in form, you didn't get picked. Nor did it matter how junior you were. If you were playing well, you made the starting eleven.

In the corporate world, we're hearing more and more about 'co-opetition' – which is what happens when competing companies put their heads together and try to make things better for all parties. In 2013, for example, Ford and GM agreed to share transmission technologies. At the time, Ford was the market leader in ten-speed transmissions while GM led the way on nine-speed. This co-operation saved both companies money, and freed up their engineers to work on cutting-edge applications like next-generation electric vehicles. Critically, the arrangement gave them both a competitive advantage over other car makers.[5]

Too much harmony breeds complacency. Writing in the *Harvard Business Review* in June 2018, Darko Lovric and Tomas Chamorro-Premuzic put it like this:

'From Kodak to BlackBerry to Blockbuster, business schools are spoiled for choice when it comes to examples of dominant market players that were jettisoned from the top by their complacency … Being happy with the status quo is a sure way to escape creativity. Any significant innovation in the history of civilisation was the product of *dissatisfied* minds: people who were unhappy with the current order of things and sought to disrupt the existing harmony.'[6]

So here's further proof that you need to reward dissident thinking. Group dynamics frequently push people towards agreement with the high-status people in the room. Nip that in the bud. Make it clear that you want fresh solutions, fresh directions, original thinking. Healthy competition between team members is great, but you've got to ensure that it is directed at producing creative solutions, not pleasing the leader. This should not become a game of 'guess what the leader likes'. The best idea should always win, no matter who it comes from.

You don't really want debate. Debate encourages people to pick a side, then fight to prove that side right. Instead, you want dialogue, you want questions: how would that solution work? What resources would be needed? How long would it take? Are there unintended consequences? Does it fit with the mission and vision? Is it consistent with values?

If you're running into stalemate, revisit the question. Is there another way to frame it? Get those who haven't spoken to speak. Make it a safe place for anything to be said, particularly by those who don't speak as often. Take meetings offsite, take them outdoors, change seating arrangements.

Shake it up!

In Summary

- Leading compassionately does not mean you dodge conflict!

- If you don't deal with your team's underperformance, someone will have to deal with yours.

- High fives and hugs alone won't lead to high performance.

- Continually strive to tackle the wrong kind of conflict in the workplace.

- Find fresh ways to harness creative conflict.

CHAPTER 16:

HIGH-PERFORMANCE TEAMS

The Best Teams Don't Just Want to Make a Buck, They Want to Make a Difference

Not long after I started out as a performance coach, I was having breakfast one morning with Michael Kearney. At the time, Michael – then the manager of the Leinster Rugby A team – was a wonderful supporter and mentor, for which I'll always be tremendously grateful. He's also one of those people who is brilliant at helping those around him to connect. So when Michael Cheika – the Leinster head coach – wandered in, Michael Kearney lost no time in introducing us.

'This is Enda McNulty, he plays football with Armagh. He's got a background in coaching and he's working with some of your players.'

This was all true. In particular, I'd been helping a teenage Luke Fitzgerald to prepare mentally for big games. He said 'Hello', but Cheika was very busy preparing for an upcoming game and he didn't linger. So much for that, I thought, but a month later, I got a call from him, asking if we could meet. He suggested a little Italian restaurant near where I lived in Dublin. I didn't know what he wanted to talk about, but I hoped that this might be the break I had been working towards. In those early days, things weren't easy. I was trying to balance playing football at the highest level with getting my company off the ground, and my brother Paul frequently had to help out with the rent.

So I did a lot of preparation that night, and the following day, I got to the restaurant early. But Michael Cheika was there ahead of me, sitting alone in a corner of the dining room. He was wearing sunglasses.

I don't think I'd ever been put through my paces as thoroughly.

'How do you build a player's mental toughness?'

'What would you do about a player who was struggling with confidence?'

'What would you do with a team that's low on self-esteem?'

'What about leadership? How would you handle a team that needs better leadership?'

'What would you do with someone who was too fond of being in the media?'

If I'd done my homework, so had he.

'I see you got a red card in one of your big games,' he said. 'You were sent off in front of 85,000 people. How can you talk credibly to my team about discipline?'

Interview? It was more like an interrogation. Two hours of relentless questioning, and not once did he remove the sunglasses.

At the time, Michael Cheika faced a very significant challenge. Leinster were seen as being all style and no substance. The team was siloed and poorly aligned. They lacked any kind of unified culture, let alone a winning culture. Cheika himself was not at all well known at the time – not in the northern hemisphere anyway. He had played club rugby in his native Australia and in France, and had played for his country at U21 level. He was appointed head coach in Leinster in 2005, having coached Australian side Randwick to a Shute Shield victory the previous year.

That first interview led to a second, and eventually, he invited me in to talk to the team and take up a more structured role in the club.

In the years that followed, Leinster went on a remarkable journey. From being an underperforming, dysfunctional team, lacking in resilience and grit, they became incredibly high performing, winning the European Cup in 2009, 2011 and 2012 and dominating domestic rugby for a decade or more.

> 'You were sent off in front of 85,000 people. How can you talk credibly to my team about discipline?'

Those achievements were matched by business and brand success off the pitch.

First In, Last Out

How was this transformation achieved?

No one thing, no one person turns an underperforming team around. It's a process, involving multiple interventions, experiences and events, all overseen and exemplified by strong leadership, by cultural architects.

The key leaders in Leinster at that time were Michael Cheika, captain Leo Cullen, players Shane Jennings, Brian O'Driscoll, Shane Horgan, Jonathon Sexton, Isa Nacewa and Seán O'Brien, and fitness coach Jason Cowman

It all began, as so many great things do, at a kitchen table. Michael Cheika's, in this instance, one rainy afternoon, with all of those cultural architects in attendance. This was a group of people who were deeply passionate about rugby and about Leinster rugby in particular. At this meeting, and at the many meetings that followed, we debated the steps that had to be taken to turn things around. These debates were often heated – and that's no bad thing. You want passionate people; you want the kind of positive conflict necessary to draw out the best possible course of action. But when you agree on an initiative, you want everyone rowing in behind it. Subsequent meetings pulled in everyone in the organisation: the squad, the leadership group, the coaching staff, the backroom staff, the business team. Everyone committed to driving the culture forward.

That first day, we began with honesty, confronting what author Jim Collins calls the brutal facts. The team was fragile and lacked resilience. They were not mentally tough.

Some players were in great shape. Others were not. Some would do their tactical preparation religiously before games and know the upcoming opposition inside out. Others would not. Some players made system errors – meaning they would position themselves incorrectly on the pitch – again and again. Some players stayed on to do additional practice once a session had ended. Others did not. Some players made sure to do their mental toughness work, others thought it was a joke and didn't bother. So you had inconsistent standards, inconsistent preparation.

The Leinster leadership group agreed that the change had to begin with them. It would start immediately with a resolution to set new standards, and to agree that we would be responsible for ensuring that they were met.

I remember, in a session with a group of young players, asking Leo Cullen for his definition of leadership. His response was very close to the Aristotelian idea that we are what we repeatedly do. He said, 'Leadership is what you do every day.'

He's so right. If you want to create a high-performing environment, it's about those daily standards, actions and behaviours.

The team agreed to adopt three new values – Relentless, Disciplined, Humble – and we made sure that the team lived those values every day. We agreed to a new level of commitment and engagement. One small example of that: Leo would routinely attend academy sessions, where young players were being developed. Why? In order to show them that the leadership at the club cared about them, in order to show that they were vital to the future of the club. There would be a one-club ethos. We're all in this together, with no divisions between junior and senior players.

It helped that we had a burning platform. In Ireland, the team had continually played second fiddle to Munster, who were perceived as having a toughness that Leinster lacked. We were getting slated in the media. Following a loss to French side Castres in December 2008, one pundit called our performance 'disgraceful, gutless, leaderless, spineless'.

The thing was, the talent was there. Leinster had some of the best players in the world. The culture just wasn't strong enough to harness it.

You need to pick the right team. If you've got people who are toxic, if you've got people who are wrong for the culture, if you've got people who won't maintain good standards, they have to be excluded.

Between us, myself and Michael Cheika created a detailed master plan to significantly improve the leadership and mental toughness in the team, to significantly improve communications on the pitch, to increase team cohesion and make sure they delivered basic skills under pressure.

The lack of on-pitch communication had been a big issue up to this point. When you get a break in play, you want the out-half talking with the scrum-half. When there's a line-out, you want good communication between the guys before the ball is thrown in. If the other team get a purple patch, you need to improve the communication. Heads have to stay up.

You have to identify where the problems are. Has someone's confidence dropped? Get in there, put an arm around their shoulder. Talk passionately to them about what needs to be done.

So many people rose to that challenge. Isa Nacewa, for example. His commitment in training and the quality of his intense, deliberate practice were incredible. So many times, I saw him alone on the pitch long after everyone else had gone, working on his skills. In particular, I remember watching him in the snow one bitterly cold day at University College Dublin, working on his high-balls with a laser-like focus. Johnny Sexton was the same. He could spend two hours after a session working on his kicking. Brian O'Driscoll was the same. Seán O'Brien too.

Shane Jennings was a key figure in that leadership team. At one early training session, Michael Cheika asked to me take a seat in the back of the stands, right up in row Z.

'Watch it from there. Tell me what you see.'

It was very illuminating. With that bird's-eye view, you could see exactly who was focused, who was driven, who was really trying ... and who was not. Shane's demeanour – even at a distance of some 150 metres from the pitch – stood out. He was first out onto the pitch, and always in the thick of the action. If he wasn't driving on a maul, or tackling, or carrying the ball, he was communicating. Driving on the other players, coaching the younger ones, calling for more commitment, more energy. Shane was also the last man off the pitch. The following day, after I had reported back to Michael Cheika, my phone pinged. It was Shane: *Can we meet for coffee?*

In the café, he told me that he'd only seen me at the previous day's session and wanted to know why I hadn't been at training sessions earlier in the week.

'Shane, I'm only contracted for a day a week,' I told him.

'I know that,' he said, 'but that's not enough. We need more.'

If you're a junior player and you see these superstars behaving like that, it's going to have a huge positive impact on you. Just as we discussed in Chapter 14: *Culture*, change works from the top down.

I began to see the whole thing coming together very early on. During matches, you started to see a new kind of resilience. I vividly remember how much the team's on-pitch body language improved. To keep yourself in peak state, you stand tall, you keep your head up and your breathing strong and regular. I'll never forget those iconic images of Leo Cullen, Johnny Sexton, or Brian O'Driscoll standing tall and resolute before the opposition.

You could see it in players on the side-line too. I remember Seán O'Brien, who was injured at the time, leading from the touchline when he couldn't lead on the pitch: encouraging, communicating, driving people on. I was hugely impressed with Rob Kearney's ability to perform consistently at the highest level. His confidence, composure and mental toughness in those pressure moments was outstanding.

You could see those lived values seeping into the culture. Training now took on a relentlessness that hadn't been there before, underpinned by rigid discipline. And the humility was there too. I remember after one tough game that hadn't gone Leinster's way seeing a small group of players chatting with and signing autographs for fans who had waited for them outside long after the game had ended.

Over that period, Leinster significantly improved their winning IQ. At the time, the accepted wisdom was that you had to lose two finals before you could win one. They blew that apart in 2009.

Leinster beat Munster comprehensively in the Heineken Cup semi-final, while their performance in the final silenced anyone who called their resilience into question. Just before half-time we gave up a six-point lead and returned to the changing rooms four points down. Within three minutes of the restart, Leicester Tigers had extended that lead to seven points. But there was no panic. A converted Heaslip try and a penalty from Johnny Sexton put Leinster three points ahead, and in the dying minutes, the team soaked up immense pressure to hold on to that winning margin. Leinster were the champions of Europe. I'll readily admit that that day was one of the greatest I've ever been part of. All of the mental preparation they had done and all of that behind-the-scenes work paid off beautifully. I remember texting Michael Cheika that evening. Two words: 'Mission complete.'

Imagine having someone on your team who would drive those honest conversations, who would help everyone to confront the brutal facts. Imagine having a Michael Cheika, someone who has the vision to see how much better things could be. Imagine having a Nacewa or a Jennings, who could inspire relentlessly. Imagine having a Sexton or a Cullen who could adopt the same growth mindset and relentlessness to drive improvement every day.

Imagine drawing all this together to create the succession of brilliant performances that Leinster has achieved since then.

Building a High-performing Team

A great team needs to know not only what it is aiming for, but why it's aiming for it. Purpose is critical to human endeavour, or at least any human endeavour worth talking about. If you can't articulate your big why clearly, if it's not front and centre every day, things are going to go sideways when the pressure comes on. And that purpose needs to shine like a guiding star. We've seen too that purpose needs to go deep. People like Seamus Mallon, who gave his entire career to finding peace, or Kako Bourjolly, who works with the street kids of Haiti, were motivated by something more than making a buck. The best teams are the ones who want to make a difference. The best teams are the ones who want to leave the world better than they found it.

Fortitude. There's a word you don't hear much anymore. It's defined as 'strength of mind that enables a person to encounter danger or bear pain or adversity with courage'. Great teams are those that display collective fortitude. They don't turn on each other when struck by failure or when the pressure comes on. Resilience is not a fixed quantity. It is a skill and it can be developed. And the best way to encourage it in your teams is to provide them with a support network, to ensure that those human connections are maintained.

The best leaders are also team players – you can't be one without the other. And the most resilient teams are those with an ability to look on the bright side. It sounds cheesy, but it's true. Without optimism, without a belief that you can overcome the obstacle, you're not going to overcome the obstacle. Why would you bring your A-game if, in your heart of hearts, you really didn't think you could do it? This doesn't mean you pretend that the obstacle isn't there, or that it isn't as big or as bad as it appears. No. You face up to the brutal facts. You have to get to know the challenge, no matter how awful. Then, you plan. Then, you go to work. You look at any successful team, you'll find a kind of courageous optimism.

You'll also find trust. Teams that trust each other are always the most effective. Teams where it's OK to fail, it's OK to try new things, it's OK to break consensus. Remember again that seminal Google study which found that psychological safety was the most important **You look at any successful team, you'll find a kind of courageous optimism** defining characteristic of high-performing teams: 'Can we take risks on this team without feeling insecure or embarrassed?'[1]

The big-picture visionary stuff has a role, but the truth is that you need to be able to execute. You've got to be able to take that vision, those values, those goals, and use them to schedule and assign tasks day to day. You need to have strong management and you need to have strong leadership. Preparation, analysis, homework. Remember Leo Cullen's definition: leadership is what you do every day.

Leaders are real people. They don't try to appear superhuman in front of those they lead. They bring their real selves to work. They are who they say they are. When they screw up, they put their hand up and say 'I screwed up'. People can empathise with vulnerability because they see something of themselves in it. It's much harder to connect with someone who never shows weakness. Being real with your team is central to establishing trust, and without trust, teams fail. Remember too that it's the leader who sets the temperature. People take their cue from you. So if you're motivated by status, there's going to be continual jostling for position on the team, and whatever you set out to do will take second place to that.

Being authentic, being vulnerable, this doesn't mean that you don't hold people to account. Being the leader means you take responsibility, and you have the tough conversations and make the tough calls if people fail to deliver or don't live up to the values you've agreed.

When it comes to picking the team, diversity is critical. Your team needs a mix of backgrounds, skills, perspectives. If you've got the same kinds of people with the same kinds of experience and the same cultural background, you're going to find yourself at a competitive disadvantage. Two things you need for innovation: the first is diversity. The second is collaboration. Great things are rarely achieved by one woman, by one man. We are at our best when we combine our talents.

Bringing Out the Best in People

Recognising the team member who has more to give is a vital leadership skill. You need to develop a sharp eye for those who are just treading water. In every team there's going to be people who are struggling with confidence, people who are giving 50 or 60 per cent, and are happy enough for that to continue. They may have tremendous potential, but you need to catalyse that potential, to give them the impetus they need to spring them out of their comfort zone.

There are so many great performers out there who, on their own, will continue to resist change and baulk at taking risks. *What if I move into that role and I'm not successful? Imagine the embarrassment! What would my colleagues think of me? My family? Better stay where I am.*

This is where the leader becomes coach. And what is coaching if not identifying potential in others, then providing the motivation and the support to help them fulfil it? It's not telling them what to do, it's providing the environment in which they are empowered to find the solution themselves. Ultimately, great leaders have to be great coaches, helping and inspiring their people onwards.

In my career, in my life, there's no experience more satisfying than seeing the excitement a person gets when they step up, take on a challenge and win. It's like a light comes on inside them. There's no better feeling for a leader than helping someone become more than they thought they could be. Helping to unlock the true potential of a team, organisation or community is incredibly fulfilling.

> There's no better feeling for a leader than helping someone become more than they thought they could be

In Summary

- Every organisation needs cultural architects.
- Bring your leadership group out to dinner and encourage an open, honest conversation.
- Leadership is what you do every day!
- There's no better feeling for any leader than helping other leaders be better than they ever thought they could be.

REFERENCES

Chapter 1: PURPOSE

1. https://www.nationalgeographic.com/environment/article/ inside-india-sand-mining-mafia (Retrieved 09/02/22)

2. Brendan McGurgan, Claire Colvin, *Simple Scaling: 10 Proven Principles to 10x Your Business* (Scribe Media, 2022)

3. Seamus Mallon, *A Shared Home Place* (The Lilliput Press, 2019)

Chapter 2: SELF-AWARENESS

1. Sarrachino *et al.*, 'When REBT Goes Difficult: Applying ABC-DEF to Personality Disorders', *Journal of Rational-Emotive & Cognitive-Behavior Therapy*, 35 (2017) 278–295

2. https://hbr.org/2013/12/the-focused-leader (Retrieved 18/02/22)

Chapter 3: OPTIMISM

1. Seamus Mallon, *A Shared Home Place* (The Lilliput Press, 2019)

2. Ibid.

3. Ibid.

4. Paddy McKillen Snr, *A Full Life* (whitefox, 2018)

5. Ibid.

6. Ibid.

7. Frank Nugent, *Seek the Frozen Lands: Irish Polar Explorers 1740–1922* (Collins Press, 2013)

8. Ibid.

9. https://www.hcf.com.au/health-agenda/body-mind/mental-health/downsides-to-always-being-positive (Retrieved 18/2/22)

Chapter 4: RESILIENCE

1. Martin Seligman, *Flourish* (Simon & Schuster, 2011)
2. https://journals.sagepub.com/doi/10.1177/1745691614568352 (Retrieved 23/2/22)
3. https://www.imore.com/apple-earnings-call-transcripts-q4-2020 (Retrieved 23/2/22)
4. https://positivepsychology.com/albert-ellis-abc-model-rebt-cbt/ (Retrieved 26/10/22)
5. Gabriele Ottingen, *Rethinking Positive Thinking: Inside the New Science of Motivation* (Penguin, 2015)

Chapter 6: NO EGO

1. https://hbr.org/2018/11/ego-is-the-enemy-of-good-leadership (Retrieved 23/2/22)
2. Jim Collins, *Good to Great* (Random House, 2001)
3. Ibid.
4. Ibid.
5. https://digitalcommons.unl.edu/cgi/viewcontent.cgi?article=1378&context=usgsnpwc (Retrieved 28/2/22)

Chapter 7: EMPATHY

1. Daniel Bryce, *Endurance: Shackleton's Extraordinary Voyage* (New Word City, 2015)
2. Ibid.
3. Ibid.
4. https://www.ibmadison.com/loneliness-epidemic-hits-gen-z-hardest-1-in-4-are-lonely-at-work/ (Retrieved 24/3/22)
5. https://www.microsoft.com/en-us/worklab/work-trend-index (Retrieved 24/3/22)
6. https://hbr.org/2019/08/the-key-to-happy-customers-happy-employees (Retrieved 28/2/22)

Chapter 8: PREPARATION

1. https://sz.thepacificinstitute.com/blog/2020/06/03/cultivate-enthusiasm/ (Retrieved 06/6/22)

Chapter 9: CREATIVE THINKING

1. https://hbr.org/2009/11/the-new-logic-of-rd-rip-off-an (Retrieved 28/3/22)

2. Kevin Roberts, *64 Shots: Leadership in a Crazy World* (Powerhouse, 2016)

3. https://hbr-org.cdn.ampproject.org/c/s/hbr.org/amp/2017/11/how-coca-cola-netflix-and-amazon-learn-from-failure (Retrieved 18/2/22)

4. Frank Nugent, *Seek the Frozen Lands: Irish Polar Explorers 1740–1922* (Collins Press, 2013)

Chapter 10: DIVERSITY

1. Stephen Brown, *The Last Viking: The Life of Roald Amundsen* (Da Capo Press, 2013)

2. https://www.canadiangeographic.ca/article/lessons-northwest-passage-roald-amundsens-experiences-canadian-arctic (Retrieved 23/2/22)

3. https://www.nasa.gov/offices/oct/feature/innovation-and-diversity-drive-exploration.html (Retrieved 23/2/22)

4. https://x.company/moonshot/ (Retrieved 23/2/22)

5. https://www.bbc.com/news/world-us-canada-49582852 (Retrieved 23/2/22)

6. https://news.lenovo.com/pressroom/press-releases/lenovo-earns-perfect-score-for-fifth-consecutive-year-in-2022-corporate-equality-index/ (Retrieved 23/2/22)

7. Ibid.

8. https://www.forbes.com/sites/frederickallen/2012/07/20/boss-gives-3-million-of-his-bonus-to-employees/?sh=40d748b23591 (Retrieved 7/9/22)

9. https://theconversation.com/you-dont-have-a-male-or-female-brain-the-more-brains-scientists-study-the-weaker-the-evidence-for-sex-differences-158005 (Retrieved 23/2/22)

10. https://papers.ssrn.com/sol3/papers.cfm?abstract_id=3617953 (Retrieved 23/2/22)

Chapter 11: COMMUNICATION

1. https://forge.medium.com/the-culture-of-personality-is-a-leadership-myth-7d44bad63cd3 (Retrieved 23/2/22)

2. Ibid.

3. https://www.theguardian.com/books/2015/jul/18/daniel-kahneman-books-interview (Retrieved 23/2/22)

4. https://maritime.org/doc/subphrase/index.htm (Retrieved 23/2/22)

5. Viktor E. Frankl, *Man's Search for Meaning* (Rider, 2004)

Chapter 12: COLLABORATION

1. Rory Best, *Rory Best: My Autobiography* (Hodder & Stoughton, 2020)

2. Ibid.

3. Dr Mary Collins, 'Rising Stars: How to Engage & Develop "Generation Y"', *IITD Quarterly*

4. https://www.theguardian.com/books/2015/jul/18/daniel-kahneman-books-interview (Retrieved 23/2/22)

5. https://hbr.org/2007/11/eight-ways-to-build-collaborative-teams (Retrieved 28/2/22)

6. Ibid.

7. Ibid.

Chapter 13: PSYCHOLOGICAL SAFETY

1. https://www.theguardian.com/business/2020/jan/09/boeing-737-max-internal-messages (Retrieved 2/3/22)

2. Ibid.

3. Ibid.

4. https://transportation.house.gov/news/press-releases/
chair-defazio-blasts-boeing-about-newly-revealed-messages-this-
is-not-about-one-employee-this-is-about-a-failure-of-safety-culture
(Retrieved 2/3/22)

5. https://itrevolution.com/lack-of-psychological-safety-at-boeing/
(Retrieved 2/3/22)

6. https://transportation.house.gov/news/press-releases/
after-18-month-investigation-chairs-defazio-and-larsen-release-
final-committee-report-on-boeing-737-max (Retrieved 2/3/22)

7. https://hbr.org/2019/05/boeing-and-the-importance-of-
encouraging-employees-to-speak-up (Retrieved 2/3/22)

8. Ibid.

9. https://www.brookings.edu/blog/education-plus-
development/2016/06/28/alan-mulally-ford-and-the-6cs/
(Retrieved 2/3/22)

10. Ibid.

11. https://hbr.org/1993/01/to-build-a-winning-team-an-interview-
with-head-coach-bill-walsh (Retrieved 2/3/22)

12. https://rework.withgoogle.com/blog/five-keys-to-a-successful-
google-team/ (Retrieved 2/3/22)

Chapter 14 : CULTURE

1. https://www.theguardian.com/football/2014/dec/04/fa-england-
dna-elite-player-development (Retrieved 2/3/22)

2. Ibid.

3. https://www.mirror.co.uk/sport/row-zed/gareth-southgate-
appointed-england-caretaker-8928242 (Retrieved 2/3/22)

4. https://www.bbc.com/sport/football/38064976 (Retrieved
2/3/22)

5. https://www.thefa.com/news/2014/dec/04/england-dna-launch
(Retrieved 2/3/22)

6. https://www.independent.co.uk/sport/football/international/england-world-cup-draw-prediction-gareth-southgate-tactics-system-a7990896.html (Retrieved 2/3/22)

7. https://talksport.com/football/393986/world-cup-2018-gareth-southgate-england-2/ (Retrieved 2/3/22)

8. https://www.telegraph.co.uk/world-cup/2018/07/11/gareth-southgate-understated-manager-has-transformed-nations/ (Retrieved 2/3/22)

9. https://www.independent.ie/sport/soccer/world-cup-2018/fixtures-and-results/family-is-more-important-southgate-backs-delphs-decision-to-head-home-37072767.html (Retrieved 2/3/22)

10. https://www.breathehr.com/en-gb/resources/culture-economy-report-2021 (Retrieved 2/3/22)

Chapter 15: DIFFICULT CONVERSATIONS

1. https://www.acas.org.uk/handling-a-bullying-harassment-discrimination-complaint (Retrieved 2/3/22)

2. https://www.cipd.ie/news-resources/practical-guidance/guides/workplace-conflict#gref (Retrieved 2/3/22)

3. https://www.smithsonianbooks.com/store/aviation-military-history/published-writings-wilbur-and-orville-wright/ (Retrieved 2/3/22)

4. https://lemelson.mit.edu/resources/steve-jobs-and-steve-wozniak (Retrieved 2/3/22)

5. https://hbr.org/2021/01/the-rules-of-co-opetition (Retrieved 2/3/22)

6. https://hbr.org/2018/06/too-much-team-harmony-can-kill-creativity (Retrieved 2/3/22)

Chapter 16: HIGH-PERFORMANCE TEAMS

1. https://rework.withgoogle.com/blog/five-keys-to-a-successful-google-team/

ACKNOWLEDGEMENTS

John Hearne, thank you for your amazing devotion to this book; thank you for your adversarial collaboration and for bringing the project to life with your own brand of literary magic. It's been very exciting to build on the success of *Commit!*, our first book together.

Mary Collins, thank you for more than ten years of collaboration, of teamship and of support on our deeply fulfilling projects here at McNulty. Katrina Steady, your contribution to this book has been seismic. We're hugely excited about continuing to collaborate with you on the journey ahead. Michael Dempsey. Thank you for your humility, your wisdom and your amazing strategic capability. Thank you, Michael, for the support – personally and professionally – through all of the highs and lows.

Eamonn Sinnott. Thank you for your friendship, thank you for always challenging my thinking to go to the next level, thank you for your loyalty and your amazing thought leadership. Brian Quinn. Thanks for being an wonderful friend and for inspiring me with your life's work and your incredible moonshot thinking. Lorraine Culligan, you've been an inspiration to me and to our team for the way you handled the pandemic, and in how you've led with such authenticity and compassion. To Bernard Byrne. Thank you for allowing us to partner with you on the voyage to IPO and beyond. Kako Bourjolly. You have made a profound positive impact on my life and on the lives of hundreds of thousands of others in Haiti. Let's continue to chase that dream of impacting positively on the lives of one million children. Ciara Doherty. Thank you for shining a light on vulnerable women and men, and for showing how that vulnerability can become a superpower. To Martin Bailee, thanks for your ongoing friendship and for your partnership on the game-changing cultural transformation at Lidl. Paddy Courtney. You continue to show how leadership in the not-for-profit sector can transform community and society. Rory Best. What a joy it has been to see you grow and develop as a leader for Ireland. What a joy to see you calm, cool and yet ferocious through those historic victories. Thanks for your great contribution to this book, and thank you for your loyalty on the amazing voyage we made with the Irish rugby team. Tim O'Connor. You have had a massive impact on my life over the last three years. I hope to continue to learn from you and to carry on your and Seamus Mallon's powerful legacy.

Nick Winkelman. Thank you for all the fun and joy we had on the pitch at Irish rugby training sessions, and for the adversarial collaboration we had in our work together. I'm deeply appreciative of your friendship and the positive energy you have brought to all our interactions over the last seven years. Eugene Conlon. Our trips around Europe together were an education for me. Thank you for your support, your loyalty and your motivational stamina. Brian McCarson. Thank you for the incredible leadership lessons on the way to Devil's Chasm. Sinead Cassidy. Your personal growth, your enthusiasm and your positive energy have been a complete joy to witness over the last ten years. John McCormack. Thank you for your wisdom, your guidance, your positive challenge and, most importantly, for the massive impact you have had on many thousands of young leaders' lives. And to Rosie Pearce and Chris Wold at whitefox. Thank you for making this book happen. I look forward to working with you again in the future.

Dessie Ryan. Dessie, you have been the most authentic leader in my life to date. My commitment is to ensure your legacy lives strong. Padraic Moyles. Thank you for your friendship, for your loyalty, for your inspiration and your game-changing mentality. Thank you too for challenging me to be the best version of myself. Michael Kearney. I greatly appreciate your ongoing mentorship, guidance, support and friendship.

To Joe Schmidt. Joe, I was so fortunate to work with and to learn from you over those ten years with Leinster and Ireland. Thank you for brilliant victories and wonderful memories along the way. Michael Cheika. Thank you for the incredible journey we went on together in the transformation of Leinster Rugby. Denis O'Brien, you saw my potential in the early days. Thank you for believing in the impact our company could have internationally, long before anyone else did. You showed us how global companies like Digicel could help to transform local communities around the world. Thank you to Feargal McCormack of FPM for your incredible advice, support and guidance over the last three years. Paul McGrane, my old Armagh teammate, my friend and our CFO. Huge thanks for your total leadership on and off the pitch.

To the McNulty team, past, present and future. Thank you for your commitment and devotion to our vision, our values and our impact. To our charitable partners, thank you for your tireless strength and bravery in the face of adversity.

And to our amazing client family in pro sport, in global corporate and hyper-growth companies. Without you, we would not be able to continue our work or have the impact that we have had around the world. Thank you for your support, your positive challenge and your ongoing drive to make a huge positive difference for everyone.